Money back guaranteed

Anna Tims

guardianbooks

Published by Guardian Books 2010

2 4 6 8 10 9 7 5 3 1

First published in Great Britain in 2010 by
Guardian Books
Kings Place, 90 York Way
London N1 9GU

www.guardianbooks.co.uk

A CIP catalogue record for this book
is available from the British Library

ISBN 978-0-85265-146-9

Typeset by Palimpsest Book Production Ltd,
Grangemouth, Stirlingshire

Printed and bound in Great Britain by
CPI Bookmarque, Croydon, Surrey

Contents

Introduction

Some 12 years ago, when mobile phones were deemed a menacing novelty and surfing required a wet suit, I began a consumer help column in the *Guardian*. At first, I saw it as a bit of light entertainment. Correspondents pondered the mystery of the 'statutory rights' mentioned bafflingly on the backs of their cereal boxes. A maggoty fish steak exposed a little-known European Commission ruling governing the quantity of invertebrates permitted per tonne of cod. Gradually, however, the picture darkened. I began to realise the sinister lengths to which companies will go to ensnare customers and the cunning they employ to ensure that customers don't get what they pay for.

We are all zestful consumers. We withdraw large sums from our bank accounts to spend on the latest plasma screen; we and our matching designer luggage jet off for holidays in tropical climes; we pledge our savings to shadowy men in Essex to glamorise our kitchens; and we pay premiums to insurance companies to safeguard our indulgences. Our lives, nevertheless, are fraught with menace. Those banks have sinister designs on our savings, the plasma screen turns out to be for ornamental use only, the designer luggage holidays independently in Luton and the new kitchen arrives in mismatched dribbles over 12 months. As for the insurance companies, so amiable in the good times, they are the first to scarper in a crisis.

– The British are not very good at complaining. Whingeing, yes. We will lament avidly to friends about poor service in a restaurant or the intimidating temperament of a new computer, but we are reluctant to do anything constructive about it. It could be that we are embarrassed to make a scene in a restaurant or too unsure of our technical skills to blame the computer manufacturer. It's more likely that we are fazed by the impenetrable automated shields that companies construct around themselves to fend off customers who call them. Companies are proud of these shields. They explain that the telephonic wizardry that swirls us round a menu of dead-end options enables them to serve vast numbers of customers who, in the old days, would have had to settle for face-to-face confrontations with a human.

It is the vast numbers that are, largely, the problem. Companies have become too big. Their structures are designed to serve multitudes simultaneously and are often incapable of accommodating individual details. Call-centre operatives tend to be more interested in ratcheting up their tally of answered calls to satisfy their supervisors than in digesting complaints that do not fit the usual mould. You can't expect them to care that your great-aunt in Tyneside has had her telephone line suspended when digital numerals are flashing above their heads showing that 400 calls are queuing.

Moreover, minions and supervisors alike consider themselves impotent in the face of that electronic tyrant The Computer. Quite how the corporate brain functioned before the days of the fluorescent screen is uncertain. Bookings have been blocked, refunds refused, orders withheld, all because 'the system won't allow it'. Two women GPs who wrote in to my column were forbidden to use their titles on airline tickets because the 'system' declined to recognise women as doctors. Another was barred for booking a flight because her name was too long. One correspondent who tried to buy three footstools from Ikea was told he could only buy two at a time on two separate days because the system would not permit more to be fork-lifted down from the warehouse. As for the refunds due to wronged customers . . . The Computer recognises that these would haemorrhage gratifying profits and so forbids its menials to obey their better instincts. 'Every attempt to repay the sum owed was thrown out by the system,' an official from Mastercare once told me sorrowfully, while the energy giant TXU explained: 'We've inherited computer systems that don't automatically send refunds.'

It is curious how often the inflexibility of corporate computer systems works to the companies' advantage. Unkind minds might even suppose that, rather than automata programmed to regurgitate a corporate mantra, customer services staff are, in fact, blessed with unappreciated creativity. For companies to remain fat and sleek, especially in times of economic gloom, this kind of inventiveness is essential. Why, for instance, should a company sell a customer one item when it can force them to pay for two? If someone tries to cancel their contract, the company can simply ignore the request and continue helping itself to the customer's money. And there is no reason why death should deprive a company of a lucrative income. The mobile phone company Orange wrote to a newly deceased customer to point out that he could not cancel his contract before his 12 months were up. 'Are you having trouble paying your bill?' it asked solicitously.

At least a legitimate contract did exist. Some firms, anxious to impress their accountants, try to pick the pockets of people who have never signed up to them. There was the case of the man who received an unsolicited handset from another mobile phone company, Three. When he alerted them, he was told that in order to return it he would have to open an account so that The System could process the operation. And my column has teemed with householders menaced by huge bills because a utilities company has made off with their account.

These customers are the luckier ones. Someone has picked up the phone and listened to their complaint, even if the response has been unexpected. Some traders protect themselves from a disgruntled public by resisting all attempts to communicate. This useful tactic is not employed simply by dodgy outfits like the removals firm whose manager told me he files all complaints letters in his waste paper bin. There was Next online, for instance, which ordered staff to delete all requests for a call-back to eliminate a backlog, and the online retailer ebuyer, which told an empty-handed customer that it had sat on her complaint for so long that it considered the matter closed and had deleted her file. Then there was the almost admirable inventiveness of the telecoms firm Homecall, which arbitrarily altered a customer's name on its records and then refused to speak to him because he was not the named account holder (although this difficulty did not prevent it from pocketing his payments).

Most reasonable people accept that things can go wrong. Computers are, by nature, highly strung, and promised technicians are as prone to vomiting bugs as the rest of us. What counts is the manner in which the company tackles the problem. Tiny details – a friendly live voice answering the phone, a murmur of apology – will mollify most disgruntled customers. But most of the letters that reach me are from people several traumatic months – or years – down the line. These reluctant adventurers have squandered half their annual leave waiting for phantom engineers. Hours of their social life have been spent obeying robotic voices on automated answer systems, writing letters that produce automated responses and dodging debt collectors baying for money they do not owe. Problems caused by small oversights can swell into terrifying sagas when big corporations choose to ignore them.

That is why, 12 years on, I am still eager to hear of malicious combi boilers, shoddy grouting and insouciant airlines. The ensuing misery is becoming familiar, but I feel the same outrage when I read of each new case. And I am indignant at the ease with which, armed with a *Guardian* letterhead, I can usually resolve them. Most companies fear an unflattering headline. And most, when confronted with their sins, are frantic to redeem themselves before the paper goes to print. Press officers, I realise, are possessed of miraculous powers that could heal the lot of nations if properly harnessed. It took 16 minutes for one to resolve a 16-week drama.

The suffering public has to battle more bloodily to get their wrongs righted. Many emerge scarred but victorious; most fall exhausted by the wayside; and some face a foe so intransigent that the most tireless campaigns get them nowhere. But make no mistake, it's always worth complaining. Reputable companies need to know where they have failed so that they can address the problem, and even if your individual case is ignored, when similarly affected customers add their voices the issue is likely to be noticed. Trading standards authorities take action when significant numbers flag up a particular firm and regulators audit complaints and, in theory, tackle repeat offenders. So when you reach for the green ink you can tell yourself you are doing it for the common good, even if a computer-generated acknowledgment is the only visible reward.

Crucial, however, is to know how to complain effectively. A torn-off sheet of notepaper scrawled with invective will get you nowhere. This book, born of years of consumer adventuring, aims to show what can go wrong and when, how to arm yourself against disaster and, should you fall victim, how best to gain the offender's ear. Read on and take heart; if you know whom to complain to, when, and how, the chances are you will achieve your aim. And once you've embarked on the journey, you'll discover a world of suspense, cunning and comedy that you'd have supposed was confined to your TV screen (in the days when it worked, of course).

1
Shopping

'Don't shop for it, Argos it!' bellowed Argos's website. And indeed, 'argossing' is quite a different experience from ordinary purchasing, as Jo Baxter discovered when she ordered a vacuum cleaner. Soon afterwards, two hypoallergenic pillows were delivered to her home. When she rang to point out the discrepancy, she was told she would have to wait several days for a vacuum cleaner (presumably the store hoped that the pillows would tide her over). Baxter asked for a refund. Not possible until the pillows were returned, replied the friendly retail giant. Baxter drove the pillows to her local store after three failed collection attempts and waited 90 minutes while money was scraped together for her refund. The delivery charge that she had paid for the vacuum cleaner had been deducted, however, and when she asked why, she was told that a delivery had been made, albeit of two unrequested pillows, and that she should pay for it.

Multitudes of Britons rank shopping as their favourite pastime. This, claim cynics, shows that we've become a flimsy-minded nation obsessed with consumer durables. It's an unfair conclusion. Most of us lack the time and the money to abseil down tropical cliff faces or trudge to a Pole. The high street, however, is swiftly accessible and can offer, on occasion, thrills, spills and perils that would test a seasoned Arctic adventurer.

The thing all shoppers must remember is that nobody loves you. Retailers want you, yes indeed, but that's not the same thing. Friendly posters lure you through those automatic doors, plump your ego, persuade you that Calvin Klein Y-fronts will propel you joyously through life's hardships. But it's your wallet that is your sole attraction. Once you've paid up big business wants you out of earshot until the next time you feel like spending. 'They give the impression that life would be so much easier if it weren't for the customers,' a wronged shopper wrote to me recently.

The high street

In an ordered world the purchasing process would go something like this: your eye alights on Desirable Object. A friendly cashier takes your order and the amount deducted from your bank account corresponds perfectly with the sum on the price tag. The delivery van turns up at the appointed time on the appointed day bearing the Desirable Object you ordered. And when you switch it on it works. There are laws to make sure that this happens. The trouble is that not enough shoppers are aware of them, and although most retailers have a dim grasp of the salient points, they can be remarkably inventive about their interpretation. Curry's, for instance told the owner of a shiny new, non-functioning washing machine that it could process a refund only if he got an 'uplift number' from the manufacturer, even though the manufacturer could disclose the necessary digits only to the retailer. And Argos refused to refund the cost of a dud telephone because, it explained, store policy allowed for the repair of only certain brands of merchandise, even if there was a fault.

When things go wrong – how to tame a retailer

Store managers are paid for their oily persuasiveness, and you need unusual sangfroid to withstand their cunning in front of a queue of customers. It's essential, therefore, to mug up on your entitlements so that you can stand your ground when you make a complaint. Print them from an official website, if necessary, and wave them in front of a recalcitrant salesperson. Merely the words 'Sale of Goods Act 1979' should cause them to pause. At this point they will realise that you know what you are talking about. If you really want to intimidate them, reel off the titles 'Sale and Supply of Goods to Consumers Regulations 2002' and 'Consumer Protection from Unfair Trading Regulations 2008', by which stage your refund should already be rattling out of the till.

Ideally, you will actually have read through these documents so that when the salesperson demands a receipt for your faulty purchase you can remind them that the law does not require it. (Many shopkeepers are oblivious to this fact; it helps, though, if you can provide a cheque stub or bank statement to prove the transaction.) And when you are told that the shop does not issue refunds after 28 days you can point out that you are allowed up to six years to report a fault.

When you can complain

It's a heady feeling when you watch your consumer might cow monoliths, but don't let the sensation delude you. You are protected only if there is a problem with the way your goods were made or sold to you. Demanding a refund because the heel has fallen of your new stilettos is not the same as demanding a refund because the stilettos rub your bunion. The law has no sympathy for your bloodied toe, unless shoddy manufacturing caused the chafing. It's up to you to make sure that the shoes fit properly before you get out your purse. Shops that do offer refunds if you made a mistake or changed your mind do so to seduce more customers, not because they have to, and in these circumstances they are justified in demanding a receipt or imposing a 28-day deadline. But if that heel snapped off for no good reason on the first day of wearing, your statutory rights should ensure that you are refunded or reshod.

Basically, the Sale of Goods Act, which enshrines those rights, states the obvious. Anything you buy must be of satisfactory quality, taking into account the price. It stands to reason that a polyester cardigan that costs £10 is not going to feel as pleasing or last as long as a cashmere cardigan costing £200. But if that £10 cardigan has a hole in the sleeve you are as entitled to redress as the cashmere wearer, unless the hole was pointed out to you before you bought it. Furthermore, goods must be 'fit for purpose' and 'as described'. So a coat sold as rainwear should be waterproof, and if the salesperson tells you that an MP3 player has 24-hour playback the law will share your displeasure if it only has 22.

In 2000 the law was relaxed to allow third parties to form part of the contract between you and the retailer. This is useful at Christmas time when Grandma finds that the saucepans you gave her are not thoroughly attached to their handles. Grandma can, in this instance, claim a replacement or refund direct from the retailer as long as you made it clear at the till that the pans were a gift. Write the name of the recipient on the receipt or invoice and get the shop to endorse it. Most traders still don't realise this right, and so if you hit resistance recite the first few lines of The Contracts (Rights of Third Parties) Act 1999 to subdue them. It's possible that the saucepan handles were in place but the salesman bullied you into buying them; he might have been cunning enough to show you a cheaper set that he secretly knew were defective so that you could be persuaded to delve deeper into your wallet for a superior alternative. Or maybe the rascal simply misled you into the investment by making flamboyant claims about your culinary needs and the powers of his product. In any of these cases you can cudgel the offender with the Consumer Protection from Unfair Trading Regulations, which came into force in May 2008 to harmonise legislation among European Union members.

Time waits for no man – not even the British shopper

The crucial thing is to report problems as soon as possible, otherwise you are deemed to have 'accepted' your deficient goods, and you lose your right to a refund. The Sale of Goods Act allows you to complain within 'reasonable' time, but it's anybody's guess how long that might be. If that stiletto heel came off a month after purchase, it's likely, unless you were fell-walking in them, that they were poorly made and the shop should repair or replace them. If, however, you wait four weeks before mentioning that your new television arrived lifeless, you are on shakier ground. Always check that new purchases function properly as soon as you get them home, no matter how tempting it might be to postpone the battle with the cardboard casings until you return from holiday a fortnight later. If there is a problem with a delivered item and it's not practicable to return it to the shop yourself, alert the retailer and set it aside, preferably with the original packaging, until it can be collected or posted. Don't use it, add your monogram to it or in any way tinker with it or, once again, you will have 'accepted' it in the eyes of the law and will have fewer rights of redress.

Don't sign away salvation

Some firms will ask customers to sign a form on their doorstep confirming that they have received their goods in a satisfactory condition. Few delivery men are going to hang around your front garden for an hour while you unpack a new kitchen and examine each plank; nor can you be expected to discover that the shelving won't fit the cupboards until someone has started assembling them. If the packaging is obviously damaged don't accept the goods; if, superficially, all looks to be ok, sign for the delivery but write 'unchecked' beside your signature. Companies want, of course, to be shot of the goods and of you as quickly as possible so that they can get on with their money-making, which is why the terms and conditions of many of them try to scare you off.

One furniture firm's website warns that if you don't have time to check the goods as soon as you receive them you must declare 'damaged' rather than 'unchecked' on the delivery form, otherwise their insurers will ignore any subsequent laments of a fault. Other companies declare that unless you scrawl 'unchecked' any faults will not be covered by your warranty. Both these terms muddle consumer law with commercial law and are a nonsense. Your contract is with the retailer: if your new purchase is dodgy it's up to the retailer, not their insurers, to put it right.

Understanding the three Rs: refund, repair or replacement

Tempting as it is to reject an ailing item and demand a better-behaved alternative, there are times when a repair is the most rational solution and a retailer is justified in offering that instead of a replacement or refund (although you are still entitled to either if the repair doesn't help). If, for instance, the back burner on your new hob plays up it would cause the retailer disproportionate expense (and you disproportionate inconvenience) to have the whole thing collected and replaced when a technician could restore it in situ. Provided they act promptly, that is. If you have to spend six weeks blundering about an automated answer system and fielding computer-generated fob-offs before the repair or replacement allows you to cook again, you can tell the trader that you want your money back – rescinding the contract is the polite term. Or perhaps a useful relative has known skills with back burners, in which case you leave the task to him and demand that the retailer refunds you a suitable proportion of the original asking price.

Passing the buck

Your statutory rights make consoling reading tucked up in bed (headboard and four legs working in synch and mattress as described), but big business, as I've said, can have a devious soul. If that technician makes it to your kitchen to deal with the back burner you have achieved a minor victory. Often the adventure starts when you try to persuade the retailer that your purchase is faulty. Report a militant computer and the 50p-a-minute hardware helpline will tell you it's a software problem, the software helpline will tell you it's a hardware problem, and you will find yourself ping-ponged between premium rate numbers until an adviser tells you to reboot and shut up. Or, as one Ikea customer discovered, if woodworm has punctured your bought-that-same-day loo seat it must have crawled in from your skirting boards while you were removing the packaging.

Amusing as it is to encourage these imaginative feats, the fact is that it is the seller, not you, who has to prove that the goods were not faulty when you bought them, as long as you report the problem within the first six months. They can't refer you to the manufacturer, although they often try their darndest to, because your contract is with them. And they can't, as some stores do, insist that you drive your defective wardrobe 60 miles to their nearest branch for inspection. It's up to them to collect faulty goods at their own expense or send a pre-paid returns label, unless it's feasible for you to waltz it down the road in a handbag.

Just as it was beginning to make sense . . .

So far so consoling. The trouble is that in 2002 a European Commission directive sought to harmonise the rights of shoppers across the Union, but because it would have required parliamentary time to implement properly it was superimposed on to existing UK law. The result: total confusion. So now, if you insist on receiving your money back within the first six months before sampling a repair or a replacement you must invoke UK civil law. This puts the onus on you to show that the fault was lurking when you bought it. If, however, you are prepared to accept either a technician or an alternative machine you should shelter under EU law, which declares that it's the retailer who has to prove that he sold flawless goods.

However there now looms yet another European Commission directive, currently under consideration. The aim is to make it easier for European Union shoppers and retailers to do business with each other without entangling themselves in the 27 different sets of regulations that govern each member country. If adopted, the directive will sweep away these quaint anomalies and cause general rejoicings in British boardrooms. Under these proposed regulations customers will lose their right to demand a refund straight off, and they will lose rights to any kind of remedy unless they report a fault within two months. Even more thrilling for British retailers will be the fact that, whereas now the customer can choose which of the three Rs (refund, repair, replacement) they prefer, these powers would shift to the trader who will be responsible only for making good faults that appear within two years of purchase rather than the present six.

Mail order and internet shopping

In the primitive past you confronted flesh and blood when you wanted to buy something. It might not have been amiable flesh and blood, but the fact was it existed before you and was obliged to hear you out if you had a complaint. Since then things have improved immeasurably. First came those pretty catalogues full of attractive people enjoying attractive household enhancements. Then there was cyberspace. Now, armed merely with a keyboard and a piece of plastic, you can gratify most of your needs from your front room. Usually the consequences are delightful for all concerned – the call-centre industry, delivery firms and you, the well-rested shopper. It's when the process falters that you miss that rubicund shopkeeper. Wringing sympathy out of an 0870 number is a uniquely modern torment.

Playing safe

One problem is that usual sense tends to flee in cyberspace. Perhaps it's because reciting a string of digits to pay for pixellated merchandise does not feel like spending real money. Before the World Wide Web we would have been wary of scantily stocked backstreet shops run by shifty-looking individuals, but now, because any dodgy outfit operating on a shoe-string can assemble a glamorous website, we part recklessly with our savings for goods that don't exist.

It is perfectly possible to do a recce of an unfamiliar

website in the same way that you would check out a shop. Forget the dazzle of the goods for a moment. If they are priced irresistibly cheaply you have to ask yourself how the seller makes a living. If it arrives at all, that £200 moped is likely to be a substandard self-assembly import from China with an instruction sheet in Mandarin. Most consumer guides will tell you to entrust yourself only to sites that have been personally recommended to you. That's all very well if you are torn between Tesco and Ocado, but possibly you are the only one in your circle hungering for a 50cc Ninja, in which case you should consult the internet community. Forums exist for almost every kind of product, so if you Google the company name you are likely to find some feedback. (Argos has its faults but its website does allow customers to rate and comment on its products.) If there's no feedback at all that might or might not be a good sign – check out the Companies House website (www.companieshouse. gov.uk) to see how long the business has been operating. A few unhappy remarks amid a welter of goodwill are par for the course, but if the feedback is overwhelmingly negative seek your bargain elsewhere. The trading standards website (www.tradingstandards.gov.uk) hosts a handy helpmeet, 'Howard the shopping assistant', which, when you enter a web address, will find out when it was registered and do a Google search for consumer comments on it.

Next, ferret about the boring small print on the fringes of the website, bearing in mind that if something goes wrong you will need to be able to contact a live human. Is there a postal address – PO Box addresses don't count – and a working telephone number? Study the logos down the margins – it's reassuring if there is one from a trade association or regulatory body such as ISIS, which imposes a code of practice on member companies and helps dissatisfied customers achieve a resolution. Sift through the terms and conditions to make sure that they are clear and reasonable. If, for instance, there is no mention of delivery charges or if the trader reckons they can't accept responsibility for goods damaged in transit or insists that you have no right to cancel an order it's time to resume surfing.

Should you get as far as making a payment, make sure that it's handled by a reputable card processing company, look out for a padlock symbol hovering at the top or bottom of the page to show that your card details will travel safely through the ether and, if the item costs £100 or more, use a credit rather than a debit card so that you are protected if things don't work out (more on this later). Then print out the webpage or advertisement describing the offer so that it can be quoted or flourished in the event of a dispute. Once you have parted with your money the trader must send you written confirmation of your order along with any other relevant information about delivery and returns.

A little more law will go a long way

This is an appropriate stage for some extra bedtime reading: the Consumer Protection (Distance Selling)

Regulations and their 2005 amendment. Regurgitated in their most basic form, they entitle you to know exactly what you are letting yourself in for when you buy by mail order. They also give you some rights that high street shoppers don't have – namely a 30-day delivery deadline and the right to change your mind and request a refund within seven working days of receiving the goods (provided that they have not been made to order or are perishable). You have to do this in writing – recorded delivery is a good idea, although email counts – and, unless they are faulty, you will usually have to pay for the return. Your refund must reach you within 30 days.

Fob-offs and how to vanquish them

In theory, your patient homework will pay off and a pristine parcel will ornament your doormat within a clutch of working days. But real life is, of course, much more exciting than that. Some companies devise their own highly original strategies for troubleshooting. My postbag contained several cases of customers whose transactions got lost in the system and who were instructed to order (and pay) a second time, upon which the original order miraculously turned up. Result: two sets of goods, two debits and a refusal to refund the second purchase until the surplus goods were safely collected, which, somehow, the companies in question never got round to doing. Still, two is better than nothing, which is what many of my correspondents found themselves paying for. The better class of company might occasionally bestir itself to mention a problem; rather more companies waited for the customers to pursue them through their telephonic queuing systems. Two years, I think, is how long one customer had waited before appealing to the *Guardian*.

If you've mugged up on the Distance Selling Regulations you'll be ready for such fob-offs. Politely and firmly, you will be able to point out that, unless you have pre-agreed a delivery date, you should expect your goods within 30 days. When those have uneventfully elapsed, write to the company setting a deadline and state that you will deem them to be in breach of contract and expect a refund if they don't comply. Quite possibly they will insist that the goods have been sent out already. Their systems tell them so and there's no gainsaying a computer. This is not good enough. It's the responsibility of the trader to get the goods to you safely and intact. If Royal Mail is off with the flu that's not your problem. Moreover, it's the sender who has the contract with the postal service or delivery firm, and therefore it's they who must do the chasing if a package goes astray.

With a bit of luck the company will be intimidated by your superior grasp of the law and will dispatch either your order or a refund – retailers tend to rely on customer ignorance and inertia to avoid tiresome obligations – but some will resort to frankly admirable customer-repelling tactics. The telephone-less and therefore uncontactable supervisor – an excuse particularly beloved among telecommunications firms – is one of my favourites. One company told a customer that she couldn't be put through to a manager because although the manager had a telephone he lacked a telephone number. Or, when sensibly you ask for the name of a manager so that you can direct your grievance more effectively, you might be told that the Data Protection Act forbids such intimate revelations (nonsense, of course). A receptionist once informed me that she was not allowed to disclose the company's whereabouts because of the Act, which, unsurprisingly, is cherished as an excuse to stall nosy customers. Firms might deny receiving your paperwork, be it your order form, your complaint letter or proof of purchase (always keep copies and send letters by recorded delivery). Even more effective is to allow the phones to ring out unanswered, preferably on a pricey automated line. If there's a sales option on the menu you should try that instead. It's startling with what alacrity these lines are answered, and if you have a manager's name to hand you might surprise the sales person into putting you through directly. Possibly, though, you'll be sent back to the unmanned customer service lines where you started, in which case it's time to get out that fountain pen.

The power of ink (as long as it's not green)

Letters, or emails, are always a good idea when a dispute looks like turning nasty. Both, as long as you keep copies, leave a paper trail that will be useful if you have to resort to arbitration. If the firm has a customer services department and your sleuthing has identified a manager, address them first, putting their name in the subject box of any email. Allow them a week to sift yours from the mountain of other laments, then, if you've heard nothing, try the managing director at head office. Online detective work should produce the address, but if not, you can get the firm's registered address free from the Companies House website. As a last resort, for a small fee, you can find out the name and home address of the company directors (contact Companies House) and target them. Possibly you will be putting pen to paper following 20 minutes' fruitless exposure to The Pogues on the company's telephonic queuing system. If so, have a drink, take a walk and, if necessary, turn in for the night before venting your ire. Complaint letters (and telephone calls) can be stern, indignant, sorrowful – but they must be polite. Insults and expletives will get you nowhere. In fact they will give customer services operatives a valid reason to put down the phone and undermine your status as the wronged party. Many companies record telephone calls, and any abuse will return to haunt you as you progress your grievance up the corporate hierarchy.

Avoid the temptation of experimenting too extravagantly with adjectives. If the company director wants a literary experience he will open a novel. People form a mental impression of the letter-writer as much from the style as the content, so if a bully, a poseur or an emotionally incontinent whinger emerges from the pages they are less likely to take your ordeal seriously. Be to the point and as brief as possible: summarise your battles so far and include all of the relevant names, addresses, dates and order numbers. At the end, inform them that unless you receive a suitable response within a specified time (two weeks is usually reasonable) you will take further action.

Just possibly you might receive an apology – compensation even. One company I contacted was so mortified by its own behaviour that it bought its victim a massage at a health club to soothe her stress levels.

Penetrating corporate silence

On the other hand, you might hear nothing at all. There was the case of an empty-handed customer who, six weeks after posting a complaint, was told that he would never get to hear the outcome of the investigation. 'We trust,' wrote the customer services manager, 'that this demonstrates the gravity we attach to issues of customer service'. Which suggests that the eerie silence that so often follows customer laments does not signify indifference so much as speechless contrition. Reassuring as this is, it's more consoling to receive a formal *mea culpa* plus the item you originally paid for. If this is not forthcoming, don't, whatever you do, simply cancel the payment. A cheque or a credit or debit transaction is a legally binding agreement to pay, and recalling it might give the trader a legal hold over you. Instead, it's time for you to invoke the law.

The Consumer Credit Act 1974 is a safety net when goods or services don't materialise or are in any way substandard. Under Section 75 of the Act the credit card company shares responsibility with the trader for the quality of purchases over £100, so if a trader in the UK or overseas goes bust or won't play fair you can demand a refund via your card issuer. You need to write a formal letter explaining that the retailer is in breach of contract and refuses to rectify matters, then you point out that the issuing bank is 'jointly and severally liable' under Section 75 of the Act. Unsurprisingly, banks do not like this piece of legislation so don't expect a cheque by return. Should they try to stall you, tell them in writing that you will take them to the small claims court unless they respond within 14 days and report them to the Financial Services Ombudsman. A lesser known comfort is that Visa International has agreed a protection scheme for Visa debit card holders and they don't have to have spent over £100 to qualify. If the trader is in breach of contract and deaf to all pleas you have 120 days to appeal to the bank that issued your card. It will investigate, and if it finds in your favour it will charge back the money from the trader's bank and pass it on to you. The trouble is that this provision is so recent and little known that banks themselves are often unaware of it, so if your bank repels your overtures, wield your favourite fountain pen until they capitulate.

When all else fails . . .

What if you are opposed in principle to credit cards and have never had intercourse with Visa? A fascinating new life experience may be about to begin. Your local trading standards office will be able to advise you on the next step. They might well be investigating the company in question (although they won't necessarily be able to tell you so), in which case your complaint will be useful evidence. They would certainly be able to point you to a relevant trade association or ombudsman, which should offer a conciliation or arbitration service, both known as alternative dispute resolution. These tend to be cheaper, more flexible and less alarming than going to court, and you get to decide which of these options you fancy. Conciliation helps both parties settle the dispute themselves. The result is not legally binding, so if you are still unhappy you can, for a small fee, try arbitration or, if that is unavailable or unsuitable, the county court. You can't do both because the decision of the arbitrator, an independent expert, is binding.

Provided your claim doesn't exceed £5,000 you can, for a fee, have your case heard without need for solicitors under the small claims procedure. However, court rules insist that you consider an alternative dispute resolution; if you don't, you may be liable for costs even if you win. You may, in any case, be liable for some of your opponent's costs as well as your own if you lose, which is why it's important that you are sure you have a strong case, but you won't have to fund their solicitor if they choose to employ one. The website www.hmcourts-service.gov.uk gives a useful overview of the small claims procedure and when to choose it.

Whatever your grievance or your preferred route to resolving it, make sure you know what you want to achieve – your money back, replacement goods, compensation or merely an apology.

Most companies will give up the fight once you get serious about legal proceedings, but sadly a county court judgment is no panacea. Even if you win, your foe may be unable or unwilling to pay up and you'll have to decide beforehand whether you are likely to be able to enforce a judgment. You can, for a small fee, find out whether they have any previous unpaid court orders by doing a search on them at www.registry-trust.org.uk. The fact is that the whole court system rests on the premise that people are decent at heart and will pay up when they are asked to do so. Some don't, however, and because bailiffs are not on performance-related pay they are not going to pursue your £300 compensation with the zest you might expect. One bailiff told me that he and his colleagues dislike serving warrants on recalcitrant parties because they can often get violent. If it comes to this you can apply to the courts for the defendant to be interrogated about his assets. They can then seize the assets by making a garnishee application against a relevant bank or creditor. Defendants who fail to turn up for the examination could face jail.

But don't despair

Happily, disputes rarely get this far. Those retailers who don't redeem themselves at the first time of asking are likely to give in once they realise that you are fluent in civil law. In this era of instant online feedback only rogues and idiots are going to risk their reputations for the sake of a deceased toaster. Moreover, if you are persistent, companies are likely to surrender, if only to stop you clogging up their in-trays. The crucial rules are to know your basic entitlements, to complain promptly and reasonably to the right people, and to build up that paper trail – invoices, receipts, correspondence and logs of telephone calls. Accomplish this and, refund in hand, you should be free to study the adventures that can befall you when you buy a service (see Chapter 2).

CHECKLIST

- Know your rights: goods must be of satisfactory quality, fit for purpose and as described.
- If an item is faulty complain as soon as possible.
- It's up to the trader to prove that the fault wasn't there when you bought an item within the first six months, unless you are demanding a refund.
- Be prepared to accept a repair or replacement when appropriate.
- If a dispute looks set to run put your complaints in writing in order to leave a paper trail.
- Do some research on mail order/internet companies before you part with your cash.
- Check there is a proper address, sift the terms and conditions for unfair clauses, look for relevant trade

association and quality assurance logos, and search for feedback on the internet.

- Use a credit card.
- Remember that you have seven days in which to request a refund if you buy goods by internet/mail order.
- Try conciliation or arbitration schemes or the small claims court if your complaints get you nowhere.

2
Buying a service

Dolphin promised a dream bathroom in its advertisements, but it's a dream from which Rajesh Mirchandani was glad to wake. He paid the company £5,000 for a new look, which was scheduled to take a team of workers one and a half weeks to achieve. Three months later he was still unable to take a bath. The solitary Romanian workman who turned up spoke almost no English. He'd been sent no plans for the work, thought that the catalogue numbers were measurements and was unable to understand Mirchandani's instructions. Within hours he had flooded the bathroom – he'd forgotten to turn off the water supply before removing the old bath. He couldn't fit the new bath because the feet had not been delivered, and Mirchandani had to chase the missing parts himself because staff at Dolphin could not understand what their Romanian colleague was saying.

Eventually, the Romanian workman brought his unqualified brother along to help. There were more leaks. The waste pipe in the lavatory was left disconnected and capped with a plastic bag. The missing parts failed to turn up as promised. A Dolphin supervisor said that the walls had been tiled

so badly they would have to be redone. The bath panel didn't
fit the bath. Leaking pipes flooded Mirchandani's neighbour's
flat. The tiling had to be done yet again, and the bath sank
several centimetres, breaking the seal and shedding some of
the tiles. A Dolphin inspector later declared the whole bathroom unstable, but it was a month before new installers were
dispatched to refit it. Mirchandani was offered a gift of three
towels to tide him over because, Dolphin explained, company
policy did not permit compensation.

There's something reassuring about buying a service
rather than goods because it (usually) involves face-to-
face communion with a living being, hopefully the same
living being whose skills you are buying. Whether those
skills are worth paying for is another matter. When the
relationship works it's a delightful experience all round.
If, say, it's building work, you get an exquisitely
embellished home and several weeks worth of musical
tutoring from your temporary companion's transistor
(ipods have yet to reach the construction fraternity).
The builder gets an exquisitely embellished reputation
as you broadcast his (or her) virtues to your neighbours.
   This utopia should be achievable if you do the
groundwork yourself. It's tempting, when you've talked
yourself into that kitchen fantasy, to let your adrenalin
propel you into rash action. You fling open the Yellow
Pages, call up the firms with the biggest, curliest
advertisements and choose the one with the cheapest
quote. All might yet be well, but the strangers whom
you unleash in your house might be admirably

accomplished salesmen with no demonstrable skills with a power drill. There are, with a few exceptions, no regulations requiring tradespeople to have appropriate qualifications, although, that said, any claims they make about their skills must be true. The trouble is that you might not get a chance to find that they are not true until they have deconstructed your plumbing or knocked through a load-bearing wall.

How to avoid the cowboys

The safest method is to employ someone your friends or neighbours have raved over, but this is unhelpful advice if none of them has recently renewed their kitchen. Thankfully the internet has removed some of the suspense of committing self and savings to the unknown. The Trading Standards Institute operates a website to help people find reliable contractors, from plumbers to landscape gardeners. Key your town or county and the required service into www.buywithconfidence.gov.uk and up will come a list of contractors, from accountants to walking-stick makers, who have been approved by trading standards officials. Trustmark, a government-endorsed standard bearer, performs a similar service at www.trustmark.org.uk. Traders earn the Trustmark logo after being successfully vetted by an approved operator, which could be a trade association, a local authority or an independent certification organisation. If they thereupon flood your bathroom or leave the job half-finished and your indignation fails to stir them, the scheme operator will take up the case on your behalf and take any necessary action against the trader. If you don't like their conclusions you can appeal to Trustmark for a review.

When is a quote not a quote

Your enquiries should produce several affable professionals eager for your custom, and at this stage you need to make sure that you know the difference between a quote and an estimate. An estimate is an educated – or sometimes uneducated – guess at how much the work might cost, and it is not binding. A mechanic might tell you that your indolent windscreen wipers will cost £50 to fix then decide on an electrical overhaul costing £200.

A quote, on the other hand, is a legally binding sum of money agreed between you and the tradesperson before you surrender car/bathroom/great-aunt Dorothy's funeral arrangements. It is vital to get it in writing . Don't be seduced by a winsome smile and an 'I'll halve it for you, love'. Unless you have the full cost of the project, including all additional expenses and VAT in ink, you are on fragile ground if there is a dispute later on. All is not lost if you don't agree a price because the law only expects you to be charged a reasonable sum. If, therefore, you are presented with a six-figure bill for some garden pruning you need only pay what you consider to be a reasonable fee (get quotes from a couple of other firms to get an idea of what this sum might be) and leave it to the trader to sue you for the rest.

Obviously, unexpected expenses can crop up further down the line, in which case these, too, should be agreed in writing. You should also secure in writing a detailed description of the works to be carried out and the start and finish dates so that it forms part of the contract and reduces the chance of the work team moving in with you for the next 12 months (one man who appealed to me had waited two years for his kitchen to be satisfactorily completed). The law insists that services are supplied within a reasonable timescale, but 'reasonable' can mean anything from a couple of days to a year. If you have commissioned a wedding dress it's reasonable to expect it to be finished before your wedding day, but a new conservatory built on to your hillside garden might take several weeks. If it's essential (and reasonable) that the conservatory is completed before your mother's 80th birthday, add the powerful little phrase 'time is of the essence' to the agreement. This will allow you to end the contract if there is a delay. If you don't add this you'll have to settle for compensation.

Money matters

This is the moment when the affable professional may ask you for a large sum of money upfront. If the project involves expensive customised materials – made-to-measure windows, for instance – a deposit is a reasonable request. Otherwise, try to avoid it. If they really want your custom they will put up with your hard-heartedness. If, on the other hand, they do talk you into it, make the sum as small as possible to give you leverage later on if the work is unsatisfactory. You could agree to pay in stages, either on specified dates or when each stage of the work has been satisfactorily completed. Your trump card, at the end, is to be able to withhold payment until any grievances are resolved, although take care here. If the tradesman gets nasty and decides to exercise a lien (the right to hold someone's property until a debt is paid), it might be better to pay up, state in writing that you are doing so under protest and seek redress afterwards. Whatever you do, send the payment to the company (if there is one) rather than handing it over to the individual contractor. And remember, never stop a cheque, no matter how aggrieved you are, because that will give your opponent a legal hold over you. You'll be grateful at this point that you mugged up on the Consumer Credit Act (see Chapter 1) because you will know that if you agree to pay with a credit card or using finance arranged by the contractor you will be able to seek your money from the credit card issuer or finance provider if the trader goes bust or does a runner.

If you get cold feet . . .

It's possible that once you've signed and sealed the deal and the contractor has departed jubilant, self-doubt will creep up on you. A small whisky might cure this.

After all, it's natural to feel nervous when you've committed your life's savings to a loft conversion. When the adrenalin has subsided, however, you might start to regret being coaxed into that Italian marbled shower room on the side. Happily, the law has predicted this and made a comforting provision for those who have signed a deal at home, at the office or in the front seat of a Skoda, provided it was not on the contractor's own premises. As long as the deal was worth over £35, the snappily named Cancellation of Contracts Made in a Consumer's Home or Place of Work etc. Regulations 2008 allows you at least seven days to change your mind once the trader has explained your cancellation rights. They should do this before you sign the contract; otherwise you get seven days starting from when they get round to it, and if they never do get round to it you have three months to back out unless the work is already under way or is customised. If that's the case, you can still cancel but you will have to pay for any work already done. The crucial thing is that since 1 October 2008 this protection applies whether or not the salesperson was invited to call on you. Previously, it would shelter you only if the call or visit was unsolicited, and a lot of consumer guides are still confused about this. If you do 'cool off' during those seven days you inform the trader in writing, and the contract is cancelled from the moment you send the letter, not whenever Royal Mail gets round to delivering it. Keep a copy, of course, in case the trader suffers from sudden amnesia and denies receiving it.

Uninvited sales people and how to subdue them

Now, it could be that you never realised that you needed a loft room, double-glazing or lapboard fencing until the moment an enthusiastic stranger arrives on your doorstep and persuades you that you do. This, predictably enough, is known as doorstep selling, and the same contract cancellation regulations will save you from yourself if you succumb to an opportunist. The most obvious protection is, of course, to say 'no'. You have to ask why, if they are dedicated professionals, they have to tout their skills up and down side roads when comrades in their trade have more work than they can handle. Steel yourself to decline or, if that sounds brutish, explain that you must consult your partner/mother/personal lifestyle manager. Perhaps you are genuinely interested, in which case ask for time to collect quotes for comparison. The moment you are told that your rare charms entitle you to a half-price offer that applies only if you sign there and then, shut the door. If you're still tempted make sure you have gleaned exactly what company this person represents, where it can be found and precisely how much the deal is going to cost you. No matter how inhospitable it may seem, don't invite them in for a cosy chat. To start with, you can have no idea that they are who they say they are; moreover, once they are expounding on your settee it might be difficult to dislodge them without signing up to their sales pitch, although regulations introduced in 2008 have made it an offence for salespeople to refuse to leave a customer's home when requested (quote Banned Practice 25 Consumer Protection from Unfair Trading Regulations 2008 if they argue).

The sales pitch could arrive in the form of a telephone call reminding you to make a will. This still counts as doorstep selling, and the same rules apply. A popular ploy is for the cold caller to ask for your bank details for their records – with predictable consequences. At least these callers are easier to silence; just decline politely and replace the receiver – or if you want revenge for the intrusion tell them you have to turn down the oven and don't come back. If the caller's spiel entices you, ask for details to be sent by post or email so that you can read them at your leisure. It's surprising how often this is deemed impossible. The point is, of course, to get you to commit yourself in the heat of the moment when your mind is distracted by your congealing dinner. To avoid such interruptions in the future sign up to the Telephone Preference Service (www.tpsonline.org.uk), which will make it unlawful for companies to make unsolicited calls to your number, unless you have already ticked a box on some form that authorises them to do so. There are online companies that claim to perform the same function but that charge a fee. Avoid them. The TPS service is comprehensive and free.

When the workpeople move in

There will come the day when you do commit yourself to a tradesperson and you hold your nerve during the seven-day cooling-off period. You have agreed costs and schedules in writing and the cement mixer is already trundling through your back garden. From this moment on that tradesperson has a legal duty of care to you and your property. Whether they are a builder, a dry cleaner or a hairdresser their work should be accomplished to a reasonable standard, within reasonable time and at a reasonable cost. They cannot, like one windscreen repair company that damaged a car's electrical system, hide behind the printed disclaimer: 'We cannot be held responsible for any damage while work is being carried out.'

If the service involves installing goods and those goods are defective or shoddily fitted, the fitter must repair or replace them. This isn't, unfortunately, a permissible reason to cancel the contract. A decent firm, which has merely had an off-day, will redeem itself without quibbling, although larger companies may want to send a supervisor round to inspect the poor handiwork. A less reputable outfit will resort to canny strategies to silence you. The never-answered mobile phone is one (the real cowboys don't give you a landline number), and cheery promises of visits that never materialise are another. It's curious how many sudden, rare illnesses strike the relatives of incompetent tradespeople, preventing them from making contact with disgruntled customers. Some might leave a step ladder and oddments of planking strewn about your flower beds to show willing. After a year or so the law will probably allow you to keep them. Others will attempt to transfer the blame on to you for being overly fastidious. Moben had, for instance, to send an inspector to assess the damage done by its installers to a customer's kitchen. 'He asked if I really needed a sink since I had a dishwasher,' said the customer, who had been left with a sink that didn't empty and a dishwasher that drained straight in to it.

If the dream turns sour

Obviously, if you order a cooker that doesn't work you can send it back or get it repaired. If you order a kitchen makeover it's not so straightforward to return it complete with grouting and demand a refund. Civil law recognises that dodgy builders may have a conscience, and so you must first give your installer a chance to make good the havoc. Tour the disaster area with pen and paper, ideally in the company of someone with basic DIY skills, and note down all the slips and defects that need resolving. Get out your camera and record the most visible horrors, then write a stern letter to the tradesperson or company, listing the problems, enclosing the snaps and giving them a deadline by which to put things right. Add that if the deadline passes without a glimpse of them you will start legal proceedings against them.

It could be that the quality of the work is acceptable but the workman has taken it upon himself to add a few expensive embellishments. That's fine if you like them and you don't mind paying the extra. It may also be fine if the surplus work turned out to be rather important – replacing a cracked pipe, for instance – in which case you can negotiate a reasonable price for it. However, if the workman's flights of fancy were unauthorised and unwanted you are under no obligation to pay for them. Your refusal could, on the other hand, land you in a tricky situation if, say, your car is in question and the garage refuses to release the vehicle until you have settled the bill in full. This is the point where you pay 'under protest' and appeal to the courts to get your money back.

Perhaps, like the couple who spent three years without central heating after a technician came to fix a faulty radiator valve, your problem is that the work, no matter how exquisite, is not visibly progressing. If you've included 'time is of the essence' on the paperwork you can cancel once the deadline is breached, but then you'll have to go to the time and trouble of finding another contractor to finish the job. If you didn't state 'time is of the essence' now is the time to do so in a letter that sets a deadline after which you declare you will find someone else to complete the work and hold the tardy tradesman liable for the expense. The chances are the courts will have to force him – or try to force him – to pay up. You might even secure a bit of compensation if the delay has caused you undue losses or inconvenience.

Finding a sympathetic (human) ear

Sadly, there's a possibility that, no matter how movingly worded your letter, the response is silence. If you've read Chapter 1 you'll know how many forms this silence can take. It's either a deliberate silence to keep you at bay or an incompetent one because your pleading letters were used as an emergency draught excluder. Before you invoke the arbitrator or the courts you could progress patiently up the line if the company is a large one. The manager ignores you, so write to the managing director, then the chief executive, then the chairman. Find out their names either by asking whoever answers the phone or, if they are coy, by ordering the company details via the Companies House webcheck service. This costs a small fee. It's worth doing because an individually addressed complaint is more likely to be noticed, and your research will show that you are thorough and persistent.

When traders play dead

Thoroughness and persistence will not, alas, win you a victory when it comes to the most intransigent businesses. When all else fails you have the same recourse as disgruntled shoppers – conciliation, arbitration and the county court. If you haven't done so already, find out if the offender is a member of a trade association or whether they are covered by an ombudsman scheme, which is a cheap alternative to the courts. The British and Irish Ombudsman Association (www.bioa.org.uk) will be able to help here. Ombudsman schemes, which are free, are meant to be used as a last resort, once you've trudged vainly through the usual channels of complaint, and each scheme is operated differently. Some make decisions that are legally binding, others only have the power to recommend, although most member companies will obey to preserve their reputations. Each ombudsman is an independent authority, unconnected with the trade they represent, and they will consider the evidence from both sides before deciding whether you are a victim or a whinger. Obviously it's easier for everyone concerned if you have a disintegrating new conservatory to illustrate your grievance; complaints against an idle estate agent or an incompetent cleaning firm can be trickier to prove.

You can appeal against an ombudsman's decision only if you can prove that the ombudsman made mistakes or if you can produce new evidence to support your case. If the ombudsman finds that the evidence is against you, a court is likely to reach the same conclusion, so this might be a good point to surrender gracefully. However, provided you formally reject the ombudsman's decision you can still have your day before a judge.

CHECKLIST

- Do your research.
- Go for companies that have been personally recommended, that are members of a trade association or that bear a Trustmark logo.
- Insist on a written quote not an estimate.

- Agree a start and finish date in writing.
- Don't pay a deposit unless you have to.
- Use a credit card where possible.
- Remember that you have seven days to change your mind after signing a contract, unless you signed it in a showroom.
- Give the company the chance to right any wrongs.
- Keep a log of your calls and correspondence. Photograph any damage or unsatisfactory work.
- Turn to conciliation or arbitration schemes or to the courts if all else fails.
- Call Consumer Direct on 0845 04 05 06 for help and advice.

3
Holidays

It should take four hours to fly from Manchester to Cyprus. In Geoffrey Wheatcroft's case it took three days. Passengers were informed that the flight would be delayed until the small hours of the following day, and they were transferred to a hotel to wait. The next day dawned without a scheduled departure time, whereupon the hotel refused to provide any more food and evicted passengers from their rooms because of a dispute over who would pay. A plane was chartered for departure the following morning, but it was delayed by two hours. Eventually the passengers boarded, missed their departure slot, waited a further two hours and were finally airborne (although cutlery, hot food and a working toilet were not). Halfway into the flight an unscheduled stop was announced, and the passengers were forced to disembark in Turkey. It was left to a British embassy official to discover their fate, which turned out to be another night in a hotel and a further delay the next morning. Wheatcroft and his wife finally reached Cyprus at 5 a.m., three days after setting off. Any hopes of using the remaining days of their holiday to recover from their ordeal were scuppered by the discovery that their five-star hotel had set up a disco, which played music until 3 a.m. beneath the couple's balcony, and the hotel lift was ailing, trapping Mrs Wheatcroft for 30 minutes, so they had to toil up four floors to their rooms in temperatures of up to 38°C. Once home, the Wheatcrofts applied to their travel company for compensation and were told that they were not eligible for any.

Given the stresses of the high street, it's small wonder that Britons hunger for sunshine and serenity far from these shores. This appetite can now, of course, be sated by a few taps on a computer keyboard, which will secure you flights, balconies and palm-fringed sands without you having to leave your desk. Old-fashioned travellers can still snuggle up with a fat brochure and leave it to a travel agent to conjure them to paradise. Never in history has the choice of destinations been so wide or so cheap with so many firms competing to get you there. In an ideal world your main torment will be deciding which latitude you wish to sunbathe in. A reliably operational aeroplane should then whisk you in the correct direction on the correct day, your hotel will turn out to be fully constructed with the promised sea view in place, and you will return, rested and vigorous, for new battles with your native retail giants.

Earthly paradise will inevitably contain flaws, however. The rational traveller will expect small delays at the airport, and the best of tour operators cannot eliminate rain or vomiting bugs or a sudden outbreak of jelly fish. It's also a fact that luggage can sometimes go astray and that promised hotel suites might be unavoidably unavailable. What matters is how the companies concerned handle these setbacks. An apology, instant intervention and compensation – be it emergency toiletries or a discount for the disappointed suite dweller – will preserve the holiday humour. If these happen you have no real cause for complaint, no matter how irritating the disruption, and in many cases they do happen – sort of. My postbag, however, testifies to the horrors that can lurk when they don't.

Know what you're letting yourself in for

When you book a trip you have several options. The DIY enthusiast will want to surf the net and book cheap flights, car hire and accommodation themselves. The cautious and the exhausted will buy a package from a travel agent to ensure that all stages of the trip are organised for them. Others might do a bit of both – book car hire and the hotel room through an agent, for example, but sort out the flights privately. Each of these options has risks and virtues. The DIYer is likely to get a cheaper, more flexible deal, but they will be pitched into intimacy with the notoriously hard-hearted no-frills airlines and could be left stranded if one of the links in the chain breaks.

The package holidaymakers may find themselves compelled to take a charter flight in the small hours from an airport halfway across the land, but they are well cushioned by the law if something goes wrong. The others may save on flights by going solo, but they must get themselves home if the carrier goes belly up.

Useful safety nets

Until the 1990s part of the excitement of foreign holidays was wondering if you would ever see home again. There was scanty protection for travellers who found that their £1,000 had bought them a crusty side room on a construction site, and if the tour operator went out of business they were stuck there. Then, in 1992, a European Union directive was adopted by Parliament and became the magnanimous Package Travel, Package Holidays and Package Tours Regulations 1992. The chief point of the regulations was to ensure that travel firms were properly bonded so that holidaymakers could get their money back if they ceased trading. The companies are now legally obliged to take out a bond held by a government-approved body (currently the Association of British Travel Agents, its subsidiary the Federation of Tour Operators, the Association of International Tour Operators and the Passenger Shipping Association). In addition, if they sell packages involving flights they must hold an Air Travel Organiser's Licence (ATOL), a financial protection scheme run by the Civil Aviation Authority, they must take out insolvency insurance, and they have to pay customers' money in to a trust where it is held until the trip is successfully completed.

Along the way, the regulations foresee and provide for

the most common sins committed by the holiday industry. They insist, for instance, that if the brochure describes a five-star hotel on the beach you have a right to expect a five-star hotel on the beach. Holidaymakers should not, as one of my correspondents did, pre-book a suite with a sea view only to discover that the hotel has no suites and is nowhere near the sea. (The travel company in question explained to me that sea views could only be requested, not pre-booked. The fact that the hotel was a bus ride inland struck them as irrelevant.) In fact, trading standards advises companies never to guarantee uncertainties such as a room with a view in case circumstances intervene and legal mayhem is unleashed.

The brochure should also be clear about prices, and the price you read should be the price you pay. Companies can impose a surcharge only if they have mentioned the possibility in their terms and conditions, and even then they are allowed to add on extra only for currency fluctuations, transportation charges and government taxes and they must pay the first two per cent of these themselves. If there is a surcharge you should be informed in writing and given the chance to back out, and the charges cannot be sprung on you less than 30 days before departure. Before you shell out you should have clearly explained to you in writing what passports and visas are required for the trip and how long it might take to get them, whether vaccinations are recommended and what travel insurance is available. Although the reminder is useful, policies sold by travel agents and tour operators are often more expensive, so it's worth shopping around elsewhere and comparing the different levels of cover as well as the prices.

Once you are signed up for a four-star week in Venice the travel company can't suddenly decide to dispatch you on a three-star equivalent in Verona without your consent, although they may well try to. If a last-minute change of plan becomes necessary you have the right to cancel if it doesn't suit or to be compensated if the new package is inferior.

When is a package not a package?

So far so reassuring, but these regulations only shelter package holidaymakers, and with current mix-and-match trips it can be hard to tell whether you've bought a package or not. The law drafters have thought this through painstakingly and decided that if you pre-book a combination of at least two elements of the holiday – transport, accommodation or other tourist services, such as guided tours or theatre tickets – then you have a package. The price should be all-inclusive. If, say, you are charged separately by the same agent for your flights you enter a grey area and you might find that the law abandons you to your fate.

Essential sleuthing

In theory, these regulations should ensure that ecstatic postcards cascade forth from all package-holidaying

Britons. Sadly, though, there is always the odd travel company that considers itself exempt from legal restrictions. It's essential, therefore, to resist the allure of those brochure pictures until you have checked out the location and the company that is offering to waft you there.

A decade ago most high streets included at least one shop window plastered with ski slopes and tropical sunsets. Behind these sat encouraging travel agents who would talk you through your desires and suggest appropriate destinations. If there was a problem, you could return to the agency and pour forth to a captive audience. Internet bookings have killed off most town centre agencies, and now would-be travellers must commune with a keyboard or in some cases a 10p-a-minute customer services number.

You are going to be consigning large amounts of money into the unknown, so you must make sure that the travel company holds an Air Travel Organiser's Licence (ATOL). This is an obligatory protection scheme organised by the Civil Aviation Authority, and it will reimburse you or fly you home if an airline goes out of business. Beware, though: if you book through an agent and receive your ticket within 24 hours you are not covered. If the travel agent does not hold its own ATOL it is required by law to book you with a firm that does, and you should receive confirmation of which ATOL you are covered by with your paperwork.

It's also wise to choose a company that is a member of a trade association such as the Association of British

Travel Agents (ABTA), the Association of Independent Tour Operators (AITO) or the Passenger Shipping Association (PSA). These vet their members, bond them and impose a code of practice on them so that, in theory at least, the company is pledged to offer you decent customer service. If it doesn't, ABTA will intervene and assess the evidence from both sides, and, should matters reach an impasse, it can refer you to its arbitration service. The PSA has a conciliation service, and AITO offers a mediation service for a fee, and if the customer's complaint is upheld it can award compensation.

Once you've chosen a likely agent or operator, make sure that their brochure, be it online or on paper, tells you exactly what you are going to get and for what price (remember to pack the brochure with your holiday clothes so that if the promised swimming pool is missing you can be sure that it wasn't a figment of your imagination). Finally, do a bit of cyber sleuthing on the hotel and the resort that look so seductive in the photos. A holidaymaker wrote in to me once because the Tunisian hotel he had selected offered bad food, surly staff, dirty rooms and a rancid beach. The trouble was that the holidaymaker hadn't set foot in the place yet. The adjectives had been supplied by other travellers who had posted their experiences on various travel forums. My correspondent, who had paid in full for a package, was understandably reluctant to sample the place for himself and asked if his booking could be transferred to a more promising hotel, but the tour operator told him he would have to pay a 50 per cent penalty. Alas for him, the Package Travel Regulations require you to experience such horrors at first hand before you can be transferred back to civilisation. They make no provision for people who get cold feet before they start their holiday, so the lesson here is to Google your destination before you part with any money. There will be feedback from someone on most resorts – www.tripadvisor.co.uk is a good place to start. Some of it will be subjective, some unreliable, and all resorts will have upset at least one contributing traveller (usually North American), but if there are consistent laments of dirt and noise you ought to resume your brochure leafings.

Paradise lost – and how to regain it

Naturally, no amount of detective work is going to guarantee you utopia. It could be that the hotel changed hands just before your arrival and that the new hands are a little less tender than their predecessors were. Or perhaps your advent coincides with the start date of major building works next door. Or the room you have been allocated overlooks a beautifully constructed but monotonous brick wall. In anticipation of this you will have packed, along with the brochure and confirmation details, a camera and a quantity of pens and paper. Your first task is to locate the tour representative whose name and number you should have been given at the booking stage and to point out, ever so politely, your displeasure. Hopefully, the tour rep will instantly offer to transfer you to another room or hotel. If they can't do this immediately you can claim compensation for your days of discomfort once you get home, but sort this out with head office rather than the rep.

Unhappily, there is always the occasional rep who regards their posting as a year's paid leave to sunbathe, and they will consider your lamentings an unwelcome intrusion. In these cases it's time to assemble your weaponry. Bed down with the brochure and note down all the delightful promises that were not fulfilled and all the less delightful realities that were omitted from the blurb. Then get out your camera and photograph the cracked and filthy shower, the dwarfish pool or the mysterious absence of sea. Get friendly with compatriots on the package (all Britons enjoy sharing a moan), record their dismay at the place and note their names and addresses if they agree to back you up should things turn nasty. If there's an affordable number on which to contact your tour operator back home, ring it. Otherwise set out your grievances as soon as you get home and send them off with your unusual holiday photos as evidence. You may or may not get a reply, and the reply may or may not contain a reasonable conciliatory gesture. If it does, accept it, because arbitrators and county court judges will be unimpressed if you don't.

Pressing your case

If there is no satisfactory response write again, setting out exactly what you want, be it an apology, a goodwill voucher or compensation. Be careful here. You will need to be able to prove that the company breached its contract with you by providing a substandard holiday (if you didn't enjoy the trip because it rained a lot or the beach was crowded, you have no case), and you'll also need to show that you suffered a loss as a result. This loss could be hard cash that you had to spend on taxis because the promised shuttle bus had been decommissioned. It could be 'loss of value' – the cash difference between the facilities you got and the facilities you paid for – or it could be loss of enjoyment (a nebulous area), in which case you want monetary comfort for your disappointment. Very rarely can you expect the whole cost of the trip to be reimbursed unless it was a disaster from start to finish.

Where does that errant buck stop?

The company from which you bought your holiday might be too busy luring other travellers to Armageddon to pay you any attention when you complain. Alternatively, it will point the finger at another firm that you have never heard of, which, it will claim, bears full responsibility for your unhappiness. Package holidays, which sound so simple, are, in fact, a delicate choreography of numerous firms, all subcontracted to each other. When all goes well you might never realise how many different organisations ensured your bliss. But when it unravels and they start blaming each other, the suffering traveller can get caught in the middle of the corporate squabbling. One victim appealed to the *Guardian* after being sandwiched between three different companies. She had booked a package to Cuba with a travel agent, but at the airport discovered that her flight had been cancelled. An alternative departure got her to Paris for her connecting flights, whereupon she found her tickets had been inexplicably voided by forces back in the UK. The travel agent blamed the tour operator, the tour operator blamed the airline, and the airline blamed the tour operator.

Many holidaymakers don't realise – and many companies like to keep it this way – that their contract is with the tour operator who masterminds the package, not with the travel agent who merely books it. No matter what tour operators may tell you, the buck stops with them. Airlines and hotels and any other providers involved in the package are subcontracted by them and have no direct relationship with the customer. The booking agent is liable only if they made a mistake with the reservations or if they put their own package together for a customer.

Putting the heat on

So your second letter has proved no more fruitful than your first. At this point ABTA will want to hear from you, provided you booked through one of its members. You will need to write to their consumer affairs department, setting out your woes and enclosing a wad of paperwork – those brochure pictures that contrived a non-existent Jacuzzi, your confirmation documents, copies of your letters to the company and, if relevant, your holiday snaps. If these show that the company has breached the association's code of conduct, ABTA will – or should – take action. It's worth remembering that the association is itself part of the travel industry and has an interest in keeping its members happy, so it might not always seem as stern or impartial as you would like it to be. If you are not satisfied with the results you can proceed to arbitration or to the courts. It's worth taking advice from Consumer Direct or from the Citizens Advice Bureau to assess how strong your case is because you will be left out of pocket if you lose.

For those who go it alone

The above, believe it or not, is the easy option. If you are one of those who would never countenance a package holiday you are pretty much on your own when a link in the chain fails. Should you favour Sheerness over the Seychelles and your hotel is substandard you are covered by the 1982 Sale of Goods and Services Act, the Consumer Credit Act (see Chapter 2) and the Consumer Protection from Unfair Trading Regulations 2008, which harmonises EU law and has replaced the Trade Descriptions Act; but if you are staying overseas and booked your accommodation directly with the hotel you are in the hands of the laws of that land, although the Consumer Credit Act may compensate you if you paid by credit card.

You are no better off if you book a hotel and car hire through a travel company but decide to get a cheaper deal on flights by booking them yourself. If you can't get to your destination because the airline goes bust, your flight is cancelled or the route is withdrawn, you may get a refund from the airline or from your travel insurance, but the hotel and car hire folk will treat you as a no-show and charge you the full amount. Moreover, you are likely not to be protected by the ATOL scheme if you book a scheduled flight directly through an airline – or if you book your ticket through an agent and receive it within 24 hours – so you will lose your money and, if you've already set off, have to fund a replacement journey home if the carrier goes out of business.

Internet booking can cannily obscure the picture so that you are not sure whether you have booked a package or not. This can happen if you are busy reserving a flight online when up pops a link offering hotel or car hire deals. As long as you pay for the whole lot on one bill you are protected under the package travel regulations, but the law has not yet caught up with this technology and so canny no-frills airlines often bill you separately for the different components. This means that you do not have a package in the legal sense, and you could lose all your money if part of the deal goes wrong. There are ATOL-registered tour operators that will let you build your own holiday and still offer full protection if something goes wrong, so keep an eye out for the ATOL logo and shop around. If you do become unstuck on a DIY package, the European Consumer centre run by the Trading Standards Institute may be able to take up your complaint.

If you must go it alone make sure that you pay by credit card so that you can battle it out with your card issuer if there is a problem and hunt down travel insurance that covers insolvency. Actually claiming on the insurance can be more diverting than the holiday, but that's another chapter.

CHECKLIST

- Be aware that package holidays are better protected than DIY trips. You could lose your money if you go it alone.
- If you are booking a package make sure that you pay a single, all-inclusive price, otherwise the law may not recognise it as such.
- Make sure the travel agent or tour operator bears the ATOL logo so that your outlay for flights and accommodation is protected if the airline company goes out of business.
- Choose a travel company that is a member of a trade association, such as ABTA, which enforces a code of practice and offers arbitration services.
- Do an internet search for feedback on your chosen resort from other travellers.
- Take the brochure or a print-out of the relevant web page with you when you travel.

- Take pictures of any visible problems and get testimony from other holidaymakers.
- Give the company a chance to put things right. Complain to the representative as soon as possible on the spot, then, if the matter is not resolved, write a letter on your return enclosing relevant photos and paperwork.
- Remember that your contract is with the tour operator, not with the booking agent.
- Involve ABTA or another trade association if two letters to the company fail to close the matter.
- If you are organising your own trip make sure your travel insurance covers insolvency.
- If you created your own package and have problems with an individual component the European Consumer Centre will advise and may assist with any cross-border dispute.
- If you are a cruise or ferry passenger and your luggage is lost or damaged the Athens Convention, an international treaty, states how much compensation you are entitled to. Rail passengers are covered by the Berne Convention, and air passengers by the Montreal Convention (see Chapter 4).

4

Planes and trains

Most British towns and villages were relieved of their railway stations forty years ago, so younger readers might be hazy about their purpose. They were part of an old-fashioned concept of travel whereby you bought a ticket from a man in a special uniform, boarded a chain of engine-pulled carriages and were whisked along metal tracks to where you wanted to go. Trains do still occasionally turn up at the stations that have survived, but gaining access requires uncommon ingenuity. To start with, you are encouraged to book advance tickets via the website thetrainline.com, which has very decided ideas about where you are allowed to travel to. Take Audley End to Hatfield in Hertfordshire, for instance. For a traveller prepared to change at Cambridge it's a simple journey, but when Christopher Dyer tried to book a ticket on the internet he was told that it was not what is known as a 'permitted route'. Nor could the clerk at Audley End station sell him a ticket. Intriguingly, however, the system had no objection to him alighting at the previous station on the Hatfield line, Welwyn Garden City. Dyer therefore boarded the train with a ticket for Welwyn and sat down opposite a notice that threatened painful penalties for passengers who travelled further than they had paid to do. Unsurprisingly, he was challenged by a conductor who found that he could not call up the route on his machine either and had therefore to sell Dyer a single ticket from Welwyn to Hatfield to legitimise his presence on the train.

When I consulted thetrainline.com press office it admitted that Audley End to Hatfield is not a permitted route for reasons known only to the Association of Train Operating Companies. The rail watchdog, Passenger Focus, however, found that the journey is allowed and rang National Rail Enquiries, which confirmed the fact. When I called National Rail Enquiries, however, a baffled young man decided that the route is permitted but that no fares are shown for it. When eventually a fare to Hatfield was found it cost half the sum the passenger paid to get to Welwyn, even though Welwyn is an earlier stop.

If you made it through the previous chapter you will have discovered that the only certain way to achieve a restful holiday is to hole up in your own bed with the television listings. The catalogue of perils that can befall unwary travellers barely touched on the planes and trains that convey them because this experience can be so uniquely exciting it deserves a chapter all to itself.

Planes

The original idea of aeroplanes was that you flew in them. Things have progressed since then, and airlines have invented so many ingenious ways of making money that they appear sometimes to have lost interest in getting you airborne. In the case of no-frills airlines in particular, a seat on a plane heading to the destination you have selected is sometimes deemed a frill to which paying passengers should not expect to be entitled.

Airlines operate to different rules from the rest of us. Imagine booking seats for a West End show and being told that you can't get in because the theatre is full. Or checking in at a hotel and having to pay extra to have your luggage in your room with you. Indeed, until 2004 passengers whose luggage jetted off into oblivion were paid compensation calculated at levels established in 1929, when £5 was a decent weekly wage. There are rules setting out carrier's responsibilities, of course, but airlines rely on the fact that most passengers are unaware of them, and at least one budget company reckons itself exempt. Ryanair once declared to me that, in defiance of international regulations, it never offers compensation for lost baggage, or food and accommodation vouchers for stranded passengers, because it's a 'no-frills airline'.

The thrill of the chase Part I: securing a ticket

Overbookings, delays, cancellations, reschedulings and lost possessions are all adventures that may await passengers further down the line, but they have to be lucky enough to have purchased valid tickets in the first place. This process is not as simple as you might think, and the internet has made it even more suspenseful. The flights you are paying for may not, for instance, exist. One correspondent tried twice to book himself on to a British Airways flight using the website Opodo and each time, as his credit card details were being verified, the system crashed. Opodo, which over the telephone consoled him with a far more expensive alternative (online prices can double within seconds), explained that the seats he had attempted to book had been removed from sale and British Airways had forgotten to update its website. Further detective work revealed that the first five ticket deals trumpeted on the website no longer existed. (The postscript is that the reader booked his tickets over the phone, then later found that they had been cancelled soon after he had hung up. This did not deter Opodo from helping itself to £962 from his bank account.)

The chief trouble with internet booking is that it makes no allowances for butter fingers. If you mistype your wife's initials, or if you double click on the wrong tag and commit yourself to two singles to Baghdad, you are likely to have to fork out a second time for a set of new tickets. So invincible is the faith of airlines in their own computer systems that any booking errors are always deemed to be the fault of the passenger. One reader was informed towards the end of the online booking process that his credit card had not been authorised. He began again (the price had risen by £80 in the brief meantime) and was successful, then two confirmation emails revealed that the aborted booking had, in fact, gone through and he had been charged twice. Another had nearly completed his booking form when a message announced that the flight was sold out. He too booked elsewhere and he too found that the first transaction had gone through after all. Neither airline would refund the passengers because, they were told, the problem must have been at their end.

Because crashing systems and mischievous error messages are common side effects of internet booking it's essential to wait and see whether you receive confirmation of a booking that aborted after you had filled in your bank card details. Most email confirmations arrive within the hour; if they don't, call the airline (if you can get through) and check whether they have any record of your attempt on their system before you try to re-book. You run the risk that the seats you wanted have sold or soared in price in the meantime, but at least you won't find yourself paying for two sets of tickets.

Similarly, if the process appears to have worked smoothly, but you haven't received confirmation by the next day, resign yourself to a 10p-a-minute customer helpline and find out what's going on. Otherwise, you might turn up at the airport on the day and discover that you do not officially exist.

The thrill of the chase Part II: securing a valid ticket

Once the confirmation arrives, read it. Re-read it. Lay out all your holiday post-it notes and make sure that the online details correspond with your preparatory scrawlings. Check that your surname is spelled right, that your initials are in the right order and that the system hasn't somewhere along the line given you a sex change. Unless the name on the booking is exactly as it appears on your passport, you may be stranded at check-in on departure day. One reader bought himself a ticket using his nickname Rob. He realised his mistake and asked to lengthen himself into a Robert, but the airline declared that he would have to pay £70 for this typing feat. He was luckier than he knew. Some companies charge a penalty fee plus the difference in the price of the tickets since the original booking (only if prices have gone up, of course; you don't get a rebate if the price has dropped), so that it can cost more to alter a few letters than to buy a new ticket. Others treat any name change as a cancellation and oblige would-be passengers to fork out for a new set of tickets. Airlines blame the enormous administrative costs of making these amendments, but a former British Airways employee wrote to me once to point out that changing the name takes about 30 seconds and involves 'typing '-1=' to delete the old name, then '-', followed by the new name and, finally, 'E' to close the booking file.

There is a fear within the industry that if passengers were not severely punished for poor typing or a change in circumstances, numbers of us would snap up cheap tickets, get the details changed and sell them on for a profit. However, the airline watchdog the Air Transport Users Council, which says that complaints about ticket reservations have nearly doubled in the past few years, is lobbying for a 24-hour rule, which would allow tickets to be cancelled and amendments to be made without unreasonable penalties within 24 hours of booking.

The hidden costs of bargains

Whether you buy tickets on the internet or on the telephone, it pays to have a calculator and an atlas at the ready. These are no ordinary transactions. When you decide on a £699 television you would expect to pay £699. There might be a delivery charge, but a figure roughly in the region of £699 should be removed from your bank account. Do not be fooled into thinking that it's like this with airlines. The cost of a return flight to Barcelona with one of the budget carriers might be £30. A thrilling deal, obviously. Any sane Briton would rejoice at the prospect of sunshine and romance for the price of a pizza lunch. However, on to this £30 you must first add taxes, fees and charges, usually excluded from the headier deals. These can vary between airlines, even those operating identical routes. Some airports even levy their own taxes to fund infrastructure, but airlines often forget to mention this. Then you are likely to have to pay a fee for using a credit or even a debit card, plus a substantial levy each way to check in at the airport. (Budget airlines want us to do it online so they can shed ground staff; Ryanair has plans to remove all its check-in desks in the imminent future so now's the time to bully your great-grandparents into cyberspace so they can travel cheaply.) If you insist on taking enough clean underwear for your fortnight's holiday you will be relieved of around £10 before you can stow your suitcase in the hold, unless you can pack compactly enough to squeeze it into permissibly minute hand luggage.

Possibly you would prefer to sit alongside your family on the flight. In that case you will be invited to pay up to £30 for a set of priority boarding passes to ensure that you can grab four seats together. This can be a good investment if you are reliably muscled and can speed up the ramps to the aircraft before the tide of passengers without passes. If a bus transfer is necessary, however, you will find yourself crowded in with non-pass-holders, and it's every man for himself when the bus doors open. One airline admitted to me that speedy boarding passes do not guarantee speedy boarding, but it argued that if they worked more reliably they would cost far more to buy. Pass-holders like the disabled reader who found herself at the back of the queue should take comfort then: the pass was a bargain.

The destination lottery

Once you are airborne (and there are many more surprises that can prevent this), you are at leisure to worry about where you are going to land. It's tempting to assume that because you have booked a flight to Barcelona you will land in Barcelona. Beware. Ryanair has been busy rearranging the geography of Europe to make its routes more enticing. The Costa Brava destination of Girona, for instance, has been renamed Barcelona (Girona), presumably to harness the appeal of the more glamorous Catalan city. The fact that Girona is in a different province, a 65-minute bus ride from Barcelona, is an unpleasant – and expensive – surprise for passengers who forgot to consult an atlas before they booked.

Amazingly, airlines can shift cities around as much as they please in order to sell a flight route, but most do it under the supervision of the airline body Iata. Because Ryanair is not a member of Iata, it can please itself, and there are no rules governing how near an airport needs to be from an advertised destination. Frankfurt Hahn airport is 80 km (about 50 miles) from Frankfurt, but as Ryanair is the only airline to use it, it can call it what it likes. It once tried to tempt Norwegians to the British capital by advertising cheap flights to London Prestwick airport (Prestwick is 400 miles from London). Bargain deals might not be so seductive when you factor in the cost of a lengthy transfer by bus or train, so, if you are tempted by a budget airline, make sure you know how far the destination airport is from the city whose name it shares.

The connection conundrum

There will be times when, no matter how desirable that city is, you don't want to go there. Or rather you don't wish to venture beyond the airport, for you have your sights set on somewhere more exotic, which can be reached only via that particular hub. Manchester airport, for instance, will deliver you to most corners of the globe, but if you want to get to Los Angeles, you will have to fly via Heathrow or another airport with Californian connections. You have two options. You might be able to buy a through-ticket with the same airline, which will transfer you from Manchester to, say, Heathrow, then put you on one of its or its associates' connecting flights to LA. Or you might find you can save yourself a three-figure sum by getting yourself to Heathrow on a cheaper flight. This is tempting . . . but risky. When you buy two separate tickets you enter into two separate contracts – even if both are with the same airline and even if a travel agent organises them for you – and if you miss your connection because your first flight is cancelled or delayed, you have no rights to a refund.

One reader booked an outward-bound ticket to the Italian city of Bologna and a return from Treviso, both with Ryanair. Before departure day Ryanair rescheduled the Bologna flight to an earlier, unsuitable date, and the passenger had to cancel the trip. However, Ryanair would refund the cost of the outward-bound leg only, not the return, because that journey was made under a separate booking and had not been rescheduled. In vain did the reader argue that he could not return from Treviso if the airline could not get him to Italy in the first place.

If a DIY connection looks too good to miss make sure that you leave multiple hours between your arrival and departure, even to the extent of staying the night if that doesn't skew the cost too much. The chances are, though, that you'll find the saving simply isn't worth it.

Life is not greatly enhanced if you do load your connecting flights on to one ticket. The airline does have to reimburse you if delays and reschedulings cause you to miss your onward flight, but they are under no legal obligation to look after you while you languish at the airport awaiting rescue. The nicer airlines might treat you to a sandwich or even a hotel bed, but they don't have to do this, and it's no surprise, therefore, that many do not. If a full belly and a night-time pillow are important to you, check the terms and conditions of your preferred carrier to see how benevolent they will be in a crisis. In fact, always read the terms and conditions, even if the thought of a night in a departure lounge excites you. Yes, they are dull and, yes, you need a magnifying glass to make out the minuscule print, but they do vary from airline to airline, and it is worth knowing what your rights and liabilities are. As a rule, the less you pay for your ticket the more it will cost you if you need to cancel or amend it, or if you get stuck on the ring road and miss the flight.

What to do when you're grounded

Even the cheapest tickets entitle the bearer to a spin through the skies, but this is not an inevitable consequence. Airlines, as most passengers will already have discovered, can alter their schedules at will; they can extinguish the route you were booked to fly on; they can cancel a departure at a moment's notice, and, to minimise the possibility of empty seats, they can book half the population of North Lanarkshire on to a single plane and discard you as surplus when you get to check-in. Almost always they are at a loss to understand your frustration, and although regulations exist to reimburse you, you often need strong nerves to prise it out of them. EasyJet once informed passengers with touching candour that, in order to maximise shareholder value, flights between Nottingham East Midlands airport and Glasgow had been discontinued. Passengers were offered a refund, and at least one accepted. Back came a puzzled email from EasyJet wondering why the would-be passenger was wanting his money back when the flight in question had not yet departed. 'Please explain in full detail the reason why you are claiming a refund,' said the same customer services that had told him his flight no longer existed.

Most airlines will tell you that they will do their very best to let you know if they decide to tinker with their schedules. If they succeed, you are not entitled to a refund, even if the new departure is several days after the family reunion that had prompted your reservation. More caring carriers will reimburse you if their change of mind inconveniences you severely, but some exempt themselves from any liability in their conditions of carriage. It's amazing how often emails notifying passengers of a new schedule evaporate somewhere in cyberspace, so that you turn up on the day to find you should have departed the previous night. If this happens you will probably be told by an unmoved official that your ignorance is your fault and that you must buy a new ticket if you want to fly. Sadly, you have little option but to comply, then to try to claw back your money on your return. It's therefore sensible to check your flight a day or two before departure so that you can be sure it still exists.

In fact, it's worth doing a little extra sleuthing and ascertain that an altered flight is not actually a cancellation in disguise as a rescheduling. Passengers have legal rights to redress if a flight is cancelled or significantly delayed, and so it's in the interests of airlines to confuse the issue. If the flight number of the 'rescheduled' flight is different and if the change is announced within 14 days of departure, it may well be a cancellation, in which case you should be offered either an alternative flight or, if you decide to give up on the trip, a refund. If you choose the former you can claim between 125 and 600 euros in compensation, depending on the distance you were supposed to be flying and the delay in reaching your destination. If you take the refund, it must reach you within seven days, not the ten weeks that some airlines consider necessary for delving into their purses.

A refund or aggrieved capitulation is, sadly, your only choice if the flight is cancelled more than 14 days before you were due to fly. Regulation (EC) 261/2004 is the weapon with which you browbeat recalcitrant officials, but this only protects passengers flying from or to a European Union airport or on an EU carrier. In addition, airlines can exempt themselves from its provisions if the cancellation is caused by an unforeseeable and unavoidable event, such as a political coup, bad weather or a security alert, and beware: they can be very inventive about which events count as unforeseeable and unavoidable.

Delays and how to survive them

The same EU regulation feeds and waters you appropriately if you are delayed for more than two hours. If you are stranded in a departure lounge from dawn to dusk you can demand breakfast, lunch and dinner and a hotel room when bedtime looms. If it's for a handful of hours, elevenses or an egg sandwich are probably all you can expect, but in either case you are entitled to two free telephone calls, emails or texts. Once five hours are up, and you've missed the business meeting you were headed for, you can elect not to travel and claim a refund, and if you have already flown one leg of your journey the airline will have to fly you back to your starting point for free. You won't, alas, be able to claim any other expenses, such as wasted hotel bookings or a missed day on the beach, unless your travel insurance covers this.

Passengers booked on international flights outside

the European Union with a non-EU carrier will have
to hope they can rely on the Montreal Convention, the
shrunken new name for the Convention for the
Unification of Certain Rules for International Carriage
by Air, which came into force in 2004 and which has
been adopted by 87 nations. The point of the convention
was to update airlines' liabilities when passengers are
killed or injured, but while it was at it, it looked at
the issue of delays and the maximum compensation
passengers can claim for 'damage occasioned by delay'.
This is calculated in Special Drawing Rights, a basket
of major currencies created by the International
Monetary Fund. Theoretically, you can claim up to
4,150 Special Drawing Rights (around £4,000,
depending on exchange rates) for a delay. A beguiling
sum, this, which ought to make hanging around airports
thoroughly desirable, but unfortunately you are never
likely to get anything approaching that sum unless you
devote similar funds to court battles with the airline.
In practice, airlines may, grudgingly, reimburse you for
out-of-pocket expenses like meals, but they rarely pay
out to console you for the inconvenience or to
compensate for the theatre tickets that the delay
rendered useless. The Montreal Convention does not
get around to examining cancellations, to the delight
of airlines, most of which exempt themselves for any
liability for consequential loss in their terms and
conditions. There is no legal time limit after which a
delay becomes a cancellation, but, in theory, fighting
spirits could argue that a cancellation is, in effect, the

same as a delay, in order to claim under the Convention. You'd probably have to do this in a court room, though.

Sequential ticketing and other adventures

I received anguished laments once from a couple who had booked a trip to the United States, including four internal flights. Later they received an invitation to a wedding in New York, so they decided to skip their planned hop to Minneapolis and buy tickets for a flight to the Big Apple. They knew that, because the tickets to Minneapolis were non-transferable, they would lose the money they had spent on them. What they did not realise was that if they missed out that leg of their itinerary, the rest of their flights, including the trip home, would be cancelled. The same week I heard from a man who had reserved seats on a British Airways flight to Nice, from where Air France was to deliver him to Corsica. Then Air France changed its schedules and brought its Corisca departure forward by seven hours, which meant it would no longer connect with the British Airways flight. He had no option but to jettison the BA leg and pay for a more suitable alternative to Nice. However, BA warned him that if he didn't show up for the outward bound departure, his return ticket from Nice would be invalidated.

Both sets of passengers were victims of the little-known and malicious rule of coupon sequencing. Airlines are implacably fastidious about order. In their terms and conditions, which, of course, few people ever read, they insist that you take all legs of a journey in the right sequence. If you don't turn up for one of them without excellent reason, the rest of your tickets will be cancelled. You might be able to get the reservations reinstated or transferred if you've paid for a more flexible ticket, but economy ticket-holders face paying a hefty fee to get their flights back again, provided they let the airline know of their altered plans in advance. The logic behind this rule is to prevent the general public from saving money by manipulating schedules. Say, for instance, that it's cheaper to fly British Airways from Paris to New York via London than it is to fly direct from London. British travellers could then buy this option, discard the Paris to London bit and spend their savings on Broadway. The lesson? Should your American hosts offer to drive you to an airport further down your itinerary to show you the country, decline. You will find yourself stranded with them until you can save up for another set of fares home.

And if it's you who must cancel . . .

It's perfectly understandable if, having read all of the above, you want to shed your tickets to the sun and flee to a caravan on Dartmoor. However, whereas airlines reserve the right to cancel and alter flights at will, they will not tolerate similar liberties on your part unless you are wealthy enough to afford a flexible ticket. Should sickness or bereavement scupper your travel plans, your best hope is to claim from your travel insurance,

although softer-hearted carriers might reimburse your
estate and your travelling companion (minus an
administration fee) if you yourself expire. Nor can you
offload the burden on to a friend; most air tickets are
non-transferable, even for a fee (honeymooning brides
beware if you intend to take your husband's surname).
Most people innocently assume that even if they forfeit
the air fare they will at least get the taxes refunded.
It's an unpleasant surprise to discover that airlines are
under no legal obligation to refund these. Some will,
if you ask, but they certainly won't volunteer to do so,
and, even so, the administration fee they will charge
for their trouble can be double the amount of tax you
are claiming.

The thrill of the chase Part III: securing a seat

It's best to stick with your travel plans, therefore, and
brace yourself for what comes next. Check-in is the
next hurdle you must overcome. At this point budget
travellers who did not pay attention to the earlier part
of this chapter may find themselves relieved of a good
deal of money when they are required to pay for the
privilege of disturbing check-in staff (you can avoid
this by doing it online) and of stowing a suitcase in
the hold. Worse – you could be bumped off. Airlines,
ever fearful of losing money, tend to overbook their
flights, assuming that a proportion of the passengers
will not turn up. But there are times when, in spite of
outbreaks of flu, road works, malfunctioning alarm

clocks and the like, every last ticket-holder turns up in departures. Those nearer the front of the queue will be invited to pocket a pleasant sum of money by way of compensation and to spend a few extra hours in duty free before an alternative flight can be found for them. If enough of them decline, this will no longer be an invitation but a command. The further down the check-in queue you are, the more likely you are to be a victim, so always be early and remember that the check-in deadline is the last time at which you must be at the check-in desk, not the time when you join the back of the queue. The majority of us suffer this injustice for the sake of the wealthy minority who buy flexible tickets, so they can avail themselves of any flight they like and change their minds without having to notify the airline or pay for the reserved seat.

As long as you have a valid ticket, a confirmed reservation, and you reach check-in on time, you are entitled to cash compensation if you are bumped off a flight, and you can ask for a full refund as well if you decide it's no longer worth flying. EU regulations reckon that the minimum you must receive is between 125 and 600 euros, depending on the length of the flight and the delay. Some carriers will offer you more to sweeten you, but, frustratingly, they are under no obligation to compensate you if their overbooking causes you to miss a family funeral or an expensive pre-booked sightseeing tour.

If you are not travelling from or to an EU airport you are at the mercy of the laws of whatever country you are in, although you may be able to claim for 'damage occasioned by delay' under the Montreal Convention.

Suitcase sagas

Let's assume, however, that you were successfully checked in, that your flight duly departed with you on it and that you landed at the airport you were expecting. This will, you hope, be the end of your adventure and now you can get on with the more mundane business of jet-skiing or boardroom summits. On the other hand, the saga could hold one final chapter. This happens when you find that you are the last living soul at the luggage carousel and that the single suitcase rotating unclaimed is not yours. A brass neck and fluency in several languages are necessary at this stage as you go in search of an amenable body who will assist you. (One of the budget airlines told a reader that its lost-property desks were unmanned because it did not employ ground staff since – you've guessed it – it was a no-frills airline.) You will subsequently discover that your luggage has jetted off on a round-the-world trip of its own. If you are lucky, this will ruin only the first few days of your trip because 85 per cent of bags are reunited with their owners within a couple of days. However, that still leaves several million bags ornamenting obscure airports round the globe.

The unhappy truth is that airlines can force you to surrender your possessions to their care but bear little responsibility if they then lose or abuse them. Indeed, so certain are they that your belongings will be transmogrified in their hands that they often ask you to sign a limited release form for awkwardly proportioned luggage such as musical instruments. This, they hope, exempts them from liability if they trash it. One carrier even forced a couple to sign a limited release form for their baby's push chair, which they then broke. Head office explained that the company could not accept responsibility for any items with wheels or handles – that is, most suitcases. Airline regulations probably overrule these terms and conditions, but the idea is to make the battle all the bloodier if you are to get the redress you are entitled to.

Some airlines will buy you a toothbrush and a change of panties there and then if your suitcase vanishes; stingier ones will wait until they have examined the receipts for each of your emergency purchases before they will pay out. Once 21 days have elapsed, bags are officially deemed lost under the Montreal Convention and the airline will have to compensate you, although it may fend you off with excuses. BMI, which managed to lose a reader's wheelchair between Nottingham and Bordeaux, told the passenger he would have to claim on his insurance. Presumably there are citizens who archive receipts each time they purchase a thermal vest or a shaving brush. Most of us, however, live more recklessly, and the airlines know this, which is why some of them mischievously ask for receipts for each item in your vanished bags before they calculate compensation. Then they will assume that you have paraded your Armani jacket around town a few times and factor in depreciation.

The maximum that the Montreal Convention allows for is 1,000 Special Drawing Rights (around £1,000, depending on exchange rates), whether you had packed the Crown Jewels or a few Primark T-shirts, but you are highly unlikely to get anything like this sum. Your travel insurer will probably be more munificent, even if you do have to pay an excess charge, but nobody will be in the least bit interested in the stress and inconvenience you will have suffered without your wordly goods. One backpacker who wrote to me was left stranded in Rome after Ryanair mislaid his tent and rucksack. His trip was pointless without them, so after a dreary night in a bus shelter he asked to be flown home. Ryanair, which still hadn't found his stuff, insisted that he pay for the ticket.

It's a comfort to know that your vanished bags and their contents will start a new life with someone else. British Airways, for instance, sends luggage to auction in Tooting if it remains unclaimed after three months (the proceeds go to charity, apparently), so there's a happy possibility that you might spot your lost wardrobe on eBay by the end of the year.

There's every chance, of course, that your suitcase will make it safely off the plane, although it may not look like it did when you packed it. Should it appear that a shuttle bus has reversed over it or that someone has pilfered your camera from inside, you must complain to the airline within seven days. There's no set figure for compensation. Indeed, it's hard to wrest any redress in the case of stolen belongings because you have to be able to prove you packed them in the first place. The company will probably guess the value of your bag and its contents, subtract a good proportion of that and pay you enough to restock at your nearest Help the Aged shop. If a valuable item has been lost or damaged they will blame you for being daft enough to check it into the hold in the first place, even if their restrictive cabin baggage allowance prevented you from keeping it with you. Again, travel insurance should prove a trustier solace.

The final solution

Believe it or not, it is still possible to fly without sampling any of the perils listed above. Given the sheer numbers of passengers in transit at any one time, however, small glitches are almost inevitable, and it's important to be rational about them. An hour's delay is a pain if you are due to address an audience of business leaders, but it would be pointless to waste ire on what is, in the scheme of things, a minor inconvenience. And if your holiday clothes do not turn up at the same time you do, you might have to sacrifice beach chic on your first afternoon, but your outrage should depend on how the airline handles the problem.

Complaints to the Air Transport Users Council (AUC) have tripled in the last two years because airlines refuse to pay the compensation that they are supposed to. Charitably, the AUC attributes this to ignorance rather than wilful neglect, and it is a fact that many carriers assume that their own terms and conditions shield them from inconvenient regulations.

When something goes wrong try to complain to ground staff while you are still at the airport and, while you are at it, find out who is responsible for your suffering. It might, for instance, be heavenly powers if blizzards at your destination airport are preventing your departure or the French unions if strikes have disabled services. You will be anxious, irate and possibly encumbered by screaming children or spouse, but do try to be winsome. The hapless being you are confronting is not personally responsible for your wrecked morning and will have good reason to stall you if you lose your temper. On the other hand, no matter how fetchingly you reason with them, this being might be suffering from apathy, a contagious condition that can affect many corporate minions, in which case make a note of their name for when you write a stern letter to customer services.

This, obviously, is the next step if your flesh-to-flesh complaint gets you nowhere. You should be able to find the email or postal address on the airline's website, and some prefer you to fill out an online form. Remember to regurgitate all necessary flight details and, obvious as it may seem, work out beforehand what you want. A *mea culpa* may suffice. If you're after compensation be clear about how much you want, although you probably won't get it all and it's highly unlikely that the airline will stump up any more than they have to under EU regulations – unless a national newspaper takes an interest! It's a good idea to quote EU Directive 261/2004 or the Montreal Convention when asserting your rights so that they know that you know what you're talking about.

If the response seems unreasonable, write again and target a more senior level, such as the chief executive. The Air Transport Users Council (www.auc.org.uk) is a comforting refuge, although it is a watchdog rather than a regulator and cannot force airlines to accept its conclusions. In addition, it can't help if your grievance is a cancellation or delay that happened on your return from another EU airport. In that case you would have to find out the equivalent body in that country, grab an appropriate phrasebook and share your sorrow with them. Send off a letter and copies of any correspondence, and the AUC may take up your cause if it is a reasonable one. (At the time of writing the government is proposing to merge the AUC with the rail and bus watchdog Passenger Focus.) If the airline still resists, the small claims court is your final hope, and the good news is that a 2009 EU regulation makes it easier to make a claim to a court in another member state (except Denmark) as long as the claim does not exceed 2000 euros.

CHECKLIST

- Factor in hidden costs when you're tempted by a budget deal. Once taxes, check-in and baggage fees and transfers from far-flung, misleadingly named airports are added it might not be such a bargain.

- Beware of organising your own connecting flights under separate bookings, even if it saves money. You will have no rights if delays or reschedulings cause you to miss an onward departure.

- Study airline terms and conditions so that you are aware of restrictions on your ticket.

- Use a credit card when you book flights so that you have some protection under the Consumer Credit Act if things go awry.

- Read and re-read names, dates and times on your internet booking form because any amendments could cost you more than the price of the ticket.

- If your booking aborts after you have entered your bank details wait to see if a confirmation comes through before attempting the process again.

- Always read confirmation details carefully to make sure that they tally with your original booking.

- Never check valuables or essentials, such as medication, into the hold. Check before you set off that your hand baggage containing these complies with size and weight restrictions.

- Remember the check-in deadline refers to the latest time you can check in, not the latest time you can join the end of the queue. Get there as early as possible to minimise your chances of being bumped off a flight.

- If your journey involves several flights make sure you take each one in sequence, or you may invalidate the remaining tickets.

- Check the Air Transport Users Council website (www.auc.org.uk) to find out your rights if things go wrong. You are entitled to up to 600 euros if a flight is cancelled or delayed plus refreshments and accommodation as appropriate to the waiting time. Compensation for lost baggage is up to 1,000 Special Drawing Rights (around £1,000).
- Always buy travel insurance so that compensation covers your losses.
- If ground staff can't or won't resolve a problem write to the airline. If that fails, the Air Transport Users Council may be able to help.

Trains

It's a curious thing: I've received hair-raising complaints about Britain's rail services over the years, but hardly any of them have concerned delays or cancellations. Perhaps it's because these have become an ingrained part of British culture, like wet summers and poopa scoops. When the rail watchdog Passenger Focus surveyed passengers in 2008 83 per cent were generally satisfied with their journeys, but only 37 per cent reckoned that rail operators handled delays effectively. (Minimalist space for luggage was the main gripe, but this difficulty is easily overcome if you make sure that your holiday suitcase is no more than 2 inches wide.)

No, nearly all the anguish that reached me was caused by tickets and the mysterious processes required to obtain them. One man was sold a ticket for a train service that did not exist, and the train company declined to refund him because, it explained, 'from time to time errors do occur'. Stranger still was the case of the woman who spent £1,209 on a season ticket, which, she was told, entitled her to commute from Coventry to London on both Virgin and Silverlink trains. Too late she discovered that the ticket was not valid on either service. Why? Because she had paid too much for her ticket. The ticket, it was explained, was valid for Virgin, but only on trains routed via Northampton. There was just one hitch – no Virgin trains travel via Northampton. Silverlink, meanwhile, had discovered that her ticket was valid – for journeys from Coventry to Rugby.

The unsolved mystery of train ticketing

The puzzle of which tickets are valid for which routes can baffle rail staff as much as their hapless passengers. Before rail services were privatised the condition that used to allow commuters to travel 'by any reasonable route' was quietly changed to 'any permitted route'. Guards no longer have the discretion to decide whether a passenger is trying it on or not, and passengers are left to work out the conundrum of what a permitted route is. One reader assumed that because 'London Terminals' was printed on his ticket he would be able to alight at Victoria station, which has been a London terminal for the past century and a half. Alas, he was told that he was only allowed to go to Liverpool Street and that the phrase 'London Terminals' was used 'in case the train goes somewhere else'.

You are pretty safe if there's a direct line to your destination or if you choose the shortest route; otherwise, you are at the mercy of the Association of Train Operating Companies (ATOC) Routeing [*sic*] Guide, a byzantine tome of rules and maps that attempts to make sense of the 6 million possible journeys in the UK. 'I saw a copy of the routeing guide once and got the fright of my life,' an ATOC official told me once. 'There are a couple of people who understand it – they wrote it.'

In theory National Rail Enquiries will be able to attempt an interpretation. The Indian call-centre operative who assisted me recently had never heard of Ipswich, but provided you approach East Anglia with especial caution you should expect an amiable relationship with the ticket inspector on the day. Nonetheless, one passenger who appealed to the *Guardian* found that his simple journey was declared a non-permitted route because the computerised system used by rail staff did not recognise it. The reason is that there are too many routes to include on screen, and this means that many less popular ones have to be calculated from the routeing guide. However, few staff are trained to use the guide. 'If a fare is not in the computer, to all intents and purposes it does not exist,' a First Great Western guard explained to me. 'Even if the operator knows how to use a manual, he or she can't use the fare as the computer won't recognise it. If this occurs we have to bodge something with the over-ride facility and then write out a report to explain the anomaly in our accounts.'

Cutting your costs

The routeing bible matters when you want to save yourself a bit of cash and travel via, say Bristol, to visit your great-aunt while making the journey from Plymouth to London. Amazingly, however, it does not prevent you from creating a bargain by buying several tickets separately for different legs of your trip. Illogical this may be, but it can work out significantly cheaper if you buy, for instance, tickets from Newport to Swindon, Swindon to Reading and Reading to London Paddington instead of a standard return from Newport to London. You don't even need to get off the train at Swindon or Reading: as long as the train passes through each of the destinations on the ticket you are breaking no rules.

National Rail Enquiries and other ticket sellers will not tell you this, of course. No law obliges them to inform you of the cheapest way of reaching your destination. They must only tell you of the cheapest tickets available for the journey you requested. Indeed, my informant at First Great Western revealed that rail staff are forbidden by train operators from recommending fare splitting. 'If a passenger wants a cheaper option, they have to know what to ask for,' he said. 'Only then are we supposed to make that option available! Many of us subvert the rules, but we have been warned in the past that if we are discovered we could be in trouble.' So, if you are facing an expensive journey, check where the train stops en route and do some experimenting with fares on one of the many ticket websites. Perversely, it can work out cheaper to buy two singles instead of a return.

Quaint anomalies like these are one of the charms of Britain's transport system. And, indeed, it used to be easier to grab a bargain by exploiting them than trying to buy a straightforward saver ticket. Before 2008 passengers trying to match a fare to a time and a route would have to blunder through the labyrinth of APEXs, Supersavers, Mega Deals and White Days, each with different price structures and restrictions – there was even the fetchingly named First Great Western First Minute Business Standard. Then ATOC stirred them into a single soup and doled out three bland options: Advance, Off-Peak and Anytime. This was meant to be a joyous revolution for passengers. If you wanted to buy a ticket any time up to a day ahead you would be sold an Advance. If you were resigned to travelling after the rush hour had subsided you could save with an Off-peak, and if you were rich enough to be flexible you could travel anytime with Anytime.

Lurking behind the logic, though, are a raft of new restrictions as the terms and conditions of the old tickets have been homogenised. Now, if the demise of your dog dulls your desire for a journey, you cannot get a refund for your advance ticket, and if you need to travel an hour later than planned you must pay £10 to make the amendment. You can't even buy a return ticket in advance; you have to order two singles, there and back, on specific trains and hope, if your holiday is a long one, that advance bookings have opened for your return date. Furthermore, it takes luck and basic psychic powers to secure the very best fares, which might be limited to two tickets per train. Most train operators open bookings for services 10 weeks in advance, but they don't have to and many don't bother to set release times. It's a perfectly normal experience to telephone a company twice weekly for a fortnight and be told that bookings have not yet opened, then find in the third week that all the cheap tickets have suddenly sold out.

The new, simplified ticketing system will not save passengers from the eccentricities of ticket websites, which have to sift through permitted routes and the wildly differing fares set by each of the various train operators. After a four-hour wrestle online a reader ended up buying four separate tickets for his daughter and himself to travel from Manchester to London. 'The site often says that there's no "cheapest fare",' he told me. 'Sometimes it asked me to choose between a "single" and a "one way". Fares appear and disappear, then start off at £360 and go down to £10. In the end my daughter had to sit in first class and get free beer and nibbles and having paid less than me in second class with nothing.'

Another reader consulted the Wales & West phone

line to find a service from Cornwall to London and was told he'd have to pay £60.20 to travel on the 18.03 from Liskeard. He was then rung back to be told that ticket wouldn't be valid on that train; instead he would have to pay £120 or travel much later. He then turned to thetrainline.com and was told there were no seats left on any of the trains requested. As a last resort he called the train operator, Great Western, which immediately supplied him with two tickets for the train he wanted and at a discounted cost of £51.80. 'Same journey,' he said, 'same trains, three radically different answers.'

If in doubt, it's safest to call the relevant train operator direct since it is more likely to have up-to-date information of its services. Moreover, you can save yourself the booking fee levied by most ticket websites if you reserve directly with the company. Naturally, there are times when it's not practical to buy in advance, in which case you turn up on the day and take pot luck. This should provide a glorious adrenalin rush. You arrive with 10 minutes to spare before the only morning service departs and join the end of a queue that has been evidently solidifying for the past half hour. The few ticket machines that still function do not offer your destination. What do you do? Industry guidelines say that you should not have to wait more than five minutes to purchase a ticket, but these are meaningless. If you board a train without a ticket you face prosecution or a penalty fare, not to mention a carriage load of passengers enjoying your disgrace. You could seek out the train guard before you board and explain your predicament, but even if they let you pay in your seat you will almost certainly be forced to buy a full-price Anytime ticket, regardless of whether you have a railcard and without any relevant discounts available to the queuers back on the station concourse.

Know your rights – or when you haven't got any

When you purchase a train ticket you enter into a contract that no boardroom would accept. If you arrive 20 minutes late for a pre-booked train you have to buy a new ticket; if the train is 20 minutes late you get nothing. If you travel further than the destination on your ticket you are liable to a penalty fare; if the train overshoots your stop you are entitled to nothing. A woman wrote to me to report that her train had, without warning, omitted her station from its schedule and sped many miles onwards to London Victoria. The train operator explained that if a service is running late it can shoot non-stop to the terminus to make up time (and flatter punctuality audits). The woman, who had consequently missed a hospital appointment, was offered £2 in recompense after spending a similar sum voicing her complaints.

A common misconception is that a train ticket entitles the bearer to a seat. A naïve delusion, this. What it entitles you to is a foothold, quite possibly with several others, in the lavatory cubicle and a minimum of recycled oxygen. You are not even guaranteed a seat if you book a long-distance trip in advance unless you specifically reserve one – and it often happens that seat reservations are not yet available if you book very early. Yes, rows of empty seats might be languishing behind the glass in first class, but woe betide any footsore passenger who perches on one without sweet-talking the guard or stumping up a supplement.

Leaves on the line

So, there you are, dangling from the luggage rack with a ticket in your pocket and someone's greyhound on your feet. You should reflect on your good fortune. You are in motion, perhaps even in the direction you paid to travel and hopefully in good time for curtain-up at your grandson's school play. Hundreds are not so lucky. Either their train did not turn up at all or it turned up so tardily that there was no longer any point in making the journey. Unlike airlines, train companies will not pamper you at Costa Coffee while you wait. Nor can you predict what kind of compensation you might prise out of them because there are 22 train operating companies, each with its own ideas of customer care. A Which? Survey found that a couple of operators offer full refunds if a service is 30 minutes late, some will stump up half the fare, and some nothing at all. Once you've been hanging around for an hour all are agreed that you are entitled to a token unless the delay was outside their control, but this token can be as little as 20 per cent of a single fare and 10 per cent of a return, unless both legs of the journey are delayed. Organised minds will check the passengers' charter of the relevant company to find out what to expect before they embark on a trip, but the sorry fact is that if only one operator works the route you require you have no choice but to submit to its terms.

Constructive moaning

It's worth claiming what you can if you are delayed – after all the British pay more for rail tickets than anyone else in Europe, so even 10 per cent might buy you a latte. You need to apply in writing within 28 days of your adventure and enclose your tickets. Companies like to compensate you in vouchers so that you can repeat the sorry experience, so if you want hard cash say so in your letter, and it's a good idea to want it because vouchers may expire before you can face the railways again or need topping up when fares rise.

Season ticket holders may be at the mercy of end-of-year audits, depending on those wildly varying passengers' charters. If the operator has met its performance targets for the route in question you might get nothing; other companies might slip you a few pennies each time you are delayed by more than 30 minutes. In the not so unlikely event that your complaint is ignored or dismissed, you can transfer your grievance to the rail watchdog www.passengerfocus.org.uk. This body can assess whether your saga was handled fairly and may take up your complaint on your behalf. Just don't bank on a result. Their kindly website is full of bet hedging – they promise courageously that they may 'make representation on your behalf' and warn that they may not be able to achieve the desired outcome.

All this excitement might prompt you to revise your opinion of airlines. At least you get a seat on board a plane. But the train lot have foreseen this kind of disillusionment and if you decide to return your unused tickets you are likely to have to pay a £10 administration fee to get your money back, even if the wretched paper fragment cost you less than that sum in the first place. And if you were reckless enough to commit yourself to an Advance ticket you will be penalised for your foresight, for refunds are not allowed. Happy travelling!

CHECKLIST

- Don't be too inventive with your route to a destination. If you deviate from a 'permitted route' your ticket will be invalid.
- If you take a direct route or the shortest route to a place it is likely to be a permitted route.
- There are now only three types of tickets: Advance, Off-Peak and Anytime. You can save a lot of money by booking in advance, but you can't get a refund if you decide not to travel.
- Try fare splitting to save money. It might be cheaper to buy separate tickets for different stages of your journey even if you don't get off the train until the

end destination. Ticket sellers are obliged to inform you of the cheapest ticket but not the cheapest combination of tickets.

- A ticket does not entitle you a seat. Nor does an advance booking. If you want to be sedentary make a seat reservation.
- If long queues force you to board a train without a ticket you will be sold a full-price fare without any discounts for rail cards or off-peak hours (or you may be fined).
- You are entitled to compensation if your train is delayed by an hour or more, unless the delay is due to events outside the train operator's control. You should expect at least a 20 per cent refund for a single and 10 per cent for a return. Some companies offer compensation after a delay of 30 minutes.
- Compensation, refund charges and other policies vary widely from operator to operator and are set out in their passengers' charter.
- The rail watchdog Passenger Focus (www. passengerfocus.org.uk) will advise on how to complain and can intervene if your complaint is not satisfactorily resolved.

5
Insurance

Combi boilers would, if I allowed it, be the sustaining ingre-
dient of my column – scores of people write in each year with
the life history of their particular model. Anyone not intimate
with these fascinating devices will suspect that the topic lacks
glamour, but they should banish such prejudices, for a combi
in Enfield unleashed a tide of events that is truly thrilling.
Tide being the appropriate word here, for Benny Mallow and
his mother were wet. Very wet. It began with a soothing trickle
from the bathroom and down the kitchen walls. Then an unexpected water feature sprang up in the loft and irrigated the
bathroom. Finally, there was a splendid cascade, which coursed
through the house and removed the plaster from the kitchen
ceiling. The source of the drama was a new combi boiler
installed by a British Gas engineer the previous month. Within
an hour pipes began leaking increasingly impressive volumes,
until finally one burst and the boiler had to be shut down,
leaving the couple without heating or hot water.

Thankfully, they had British Gas's full plumbing and drainage
cover with its reassuringly elaborate promises. Its documents
were an enjoyable fiction, however, because British Gas

declared that the pipes were old and that it would only touch new ones. Mallow reckoned that increased water pressure caused by the installation was to blame, but British Gas insisted that he must stump up the £6,000 cost of repairs. Eventually, after the press office was invoked, the company agreed to fund the repairs and discovered that the culprit was the installations technician, who capped off the piping that then leaked.

Altruism is the foundation of the insurance industry. In return for a small amount of money paid by the policy-holder, insurers promise to shell out large sums if things go wrong. The trouble is that nothing ever does go wrong in the radiant universe inhabited by insurance men. If disaster should strike, these masters of spin either reinterpret it to explain the damage away, or they mire the victim in such a mesh of bureaucracy that it is almost impossible to prove a claim. One company evidently considered the Asian tsunami a media fantasy, since a survivor whose hotel room was swept out to sea was asked to provide a police report when he tried to claim for his belongings.

Extended warranties and the unpeaceful mind

Insurance is, clearly, a necessary part of life. Mortgage lenders will disown you if you don't insure your house, and you face a distressing fine if you drive without cover. Travel insurance is not yet compulsory, but perhaps it ought to be because you would be nuts to set foot overseas without it (even if trying to claim on it proves more exciting than the trip). However, the cunning minds within the industry have realised how much more money is to be made from persuading people that they need protecting from everyday trivialities. 'Peace of Mind' is how they package it – an undeniably seductive treasure, which in these progressive times can be purchased for a few pounds a week. Extended warranties are the scientific term. Electrical goods retailers can make far more profit from these than from the goods they sell, and sales staff are often paid commission for each policy they manage to off-load.

It happens like this. You want a washing machine. The sales person talks you through the astonishing capabilities of the most expensive model on offer. You agree to buy it, whereupon the same salesperson recounts the many expensive ailments that may afflict it. Probably they will flourish alarming graphs showing how many washing machines misbehave once they are in residence. At this stage the future looks so threatening that you agree to spend half as much again on an extended warranty to cover the repairs.

The sales pitch may be more subtle than this. One well-known electrical chain store tells customers that if they do not take out a warranty they will be at the mercy of the manufacturer should a fault develop more than 28 days after purchase. This is an illegal get-out because the Sales of Goods Act obliges retailers to sort out any problems that arise within the first few months, even years. Some companies lure their prey with promises of cash back if no claims are made within a certain time limit. This time limit is usually lengthy, the idea being that the customers will have long since forgotten about the deal or mislaid the paperwork before it has elapsed. Exasperatingly for big business, some customers have infallible filing systems and write at the appointed date demanding their dues. There are two solutions: to pay up (some firms presumably do) or to insist on such a complexity of paperwork, all of which then gets 'lost' in the post, that said customers give up the fight – or contact the *Guardian*.

No matter what method seduces you, you will probably regret the investment because extended warranties are rarely worth the money. To start with, nothing should go wrong with a new appliance within a typical warranty period – around three years – and if it does your statutory rights should protect you provided it wasn't your shoddy housekeeping that injured it. When your machine starts washing your kitchen floor instead of your clothes after six months the retailer has a duty to repair or replace it provided that your mistreatment didn't cause the problem. Even if, a couple of years down the line, something does go wrong and the retailer can no longer reasonably be held liable, it will probably be cheaper to fund a one-off repair or even buy a replacement than to have paid out monthly insurance premiums for two years.

People of fragile temperament might yet deem these worth the money. On paper at least they promise an obliging technician who will appear at the first sign of trouble and fix the problem for no extra charge. No more squinting through Yellow Pages at midnight and a certain freedom from dodgy amateurs and call-out charges. There is a catch, though. Well, actually, a lot of catches. For after persuading us in large rainbow type of the dastardly fate that awaits us if we don't buy Peace of Mind, the same insurers draw up lists of reasons why they won't help when the worst does happen (usually whispered in microscopic letters of faded grey). A reader who paid for a cover-plan operated by the Dixons Group to insure her new palm top was told when it developed a fault that the policy provided only for theft or accidental damage (actually, they added, her particular cover didn't cover palm tops at all). Another who had been sold expensive insurance when she bought a camera found, when she claimed on it, that her policy was invalid because the gadget had cost 1p less than the qualifying threshold.

Insurers do have hearts and there are occasions when they will concede that your claim is a valid one, but they have perfected a menu of tricks to stave off the day when they will actually have to shell out. Policies that promise a technician within 24 hours do often result in a technician within 24 hours. But note the wording: 'technician' not 'repair'. An affable individual may indeed drive a van to your premises and poke around inside your washing machine, but the chances are he won't have the necessary parts on him (what exactly technicians do carry in those vans is a mystery). He will then vanish, days will elapse, during which your clothes grow grubbier and your phone bill gets larger and you will be told that the company is having problems sourcing an extremely rare spare part that exists only in eastern Bulgaria.

The law is no friend in this instance since it doesn't specify how long a repair should take under an extended warranty. This is the point where some companies get really crafty. PC World promised a reader a replacement computer under her warranty agreement when hers stopped functioning. The first replacement was never ordered, the second was sent to the wrong address, and the store blamed shipping delay for the non-arrival of the third. This incompetence lasted six months, towards the end of which the woman's warranty expired and PC World declared that she would have to fund the replacement herself. This is by no means an uncommon excuse. The sheer cheek of it might incapacitate you briefly, but it doesn't require a legal mind to know that if a valid claim is made within the life of a warranty that claim should be honoured even if the policy expires before the firm gets around to redress.

If you have a nervous disposition you might be inclined towards a warranty, but don't let the salesperson fluster you. Retailers must keep any warranty offer, complete with promised discounts, open for up to 30 days following a purchase of electrical goods. They must then allow you in writing 45 days in which to change your mind and claim a full refund. Make sure you read the terms and conditions, especially the numerous exclusions, before signing and bear in mind that you don't have to buy a policy offered by the store you shopped in. You can hunt around for a more suitable – and cheaper policy – including those that insure every electrical appliance in the kitchen.

The Payment Protection delusion

Extended warranties have a good deal in common with that other profit-booster beloved of big business, Payment Protection Insurance (PPI), and indeed both have been targeted by statutory regulators more than once, which should put you on the alert. With PPI, instead of purchasing back-up should your white goods fall sick, you are ensuring help with a loan repayment should injury, sickness or redundancy evaporate your income. And, like warranties, PPI is usually pressed upon you as part of a package when you take out a loan or sign a credit agreement.

There are other fetching similarities. As with extended warranties, you are likely to spend far more funding your PPI than you will reap if the worst happens; you may find yourself paying out for protection that you are already entitled to; and, if you do make a claim, the insurer is likely to present a breathtaking variety of reasons why your particular misfortune doesn't count. Stress-related illnesses and back pain, for instance, don't go down well with PPI providers. Why? Because too many of us are prone to them and would cost them money. And if you have a medical condition when you take out the insurance, even something unthreatening such as eczema, you won't be covered for anything that could be related to it. An investigation by the consumer organisation Which? found that a third of PPI policy-holders might not get the benefits they have paid for because convoluted small print disqualifies them.

It gets worse. Most PPIs are paid in a single premium, which is added as a lump sum to your loan. This means that you pay interest on the premium as well as the amount you have borrowed, and given that most policies last only five years you could end up paying interest on expired insurance if your loan outlasts it. Because of this arrangement PPI policies are notoriously tricky to cancel. All this should be explained to you before you agree to sign up. If it wasn't, then it was mis-sold to you and you should complain to the loan provider who talked you into it. They will point out soothingly that everything was set out in print after you signed up and that you were given 14 days to change your mind. Don't be cowed. The dark side of the policy should have been revealed before you let the sales staff persuade you to sign up, and if the company won't acknowledge that you should turn to the Financial Services Ombudsman, of which more later.

Obviously some kind of security is desirable if a medical catastrophe prevents you from earning, and if you feel you need more than state benefits will provide then income insurance to cover all your outgoings is a far better and no more expensive option. The Financial Services Authority (FSA) has a good overview of what's out there on its consumer website www.moneymadeclear.fsa.gov.uk.

The virtuous insurer and how to unearth it

Extended warranties and Payment Protection are frivolities to be approached with scepticism. Other forms of insurance are essential, and yet most of us sign up to the first policy that wanders our way. Shopping around for the most suitable cover ought to be as fulfilling as seeking out a new winter coat: all the varied and uplifting colours of the promotional leaflets, the thrilling promises bellowed in bombastic font, the spot-the-differences in the terms and conditions and the awesome diversity of prices. When you're booking a trip the travel company will probably invite you to insure your health and belongings through themselves, and it is a temptation to accept and have the cost consolingly masked by the rest of the holiday bill. In all likelihood, however, you will find an option elsewhere that will save you the cost of a week's beer and may offer better cover.

There are numerous websites that compare insurance deals, and these are a good way to get an idea of what's out there. Bear in mind, however, that they don't cover every firm and every policy, and some big players might not be represented at all. Moreover, once you have keyed in your circumstances and requirements they will usually forward these to the broker or insurer of your choice, so make sure that the details are correct before committing yourself. Unless you are buying insurance as part of a package holiday, the insurance firm or broker must present you with a list of key facts about the policy before you sign up. This should tell you, among other things, the special virtues of that particular cover as well as any important exclusions. It should also make clear your rights to cancel. Provided that you did the deed anywhere except on the insurer's premises, you are permitted seven working days in which to change your mind, although most general policies allow at least 14 days.

Clearly, browsing Lonely Planet is a far more engaging prelude to a trip than squinting through small print, and it's normal to lose consciousness before getting to the end of the latter. However, it is vital that you know whether you will be covered if you try a spot of deep sea diving or lose your wedding ring on the slopes of the Eiger. Most of us assume that if we fall ill on holiday our insurance will nurse us back to health and home; not many realise that policies tend, for instance, to exclude mental illness, even if a breakdown is unprecedented and requires hospital treatment.

Insurance companies can be inventive about the events they will and will not cover, so never assume a standard when choosing between policies and don't be beguiled by price alone. If something is cheap it probably dooms you to huge excess charges – some insurers charge a separate excess sum for each clause in the policy rather than one overall sum, or skimp on payouts. Travellers should be covered for at least £1 million worth of medical bills and £1,500 for lost luggage. Possibly you have a rare skin condition or for reasons best known to yourself wish to carry a small Picasso on your trip to the Costas, in which case you would be better off applying through a broker who, for a commission, will search out appropriate cover, which might not be generally available.

Most firms that sell or provide insurance have to be regulated by the Financial Services Authority (FSA) or be an agent of a regulated firm, so, to be on the safe side, check that your preferred company is on the FSA register (www.fsa.gov.uk/register/home.do). Better still, check that it's not one of the unauthorised firms listed there as a warning. If you should fall into the hands of someone who is not FSA vetted you won't have recourse to the authority's complaints procedures should something go wrong.

The biological cost (if you're female or gay)

Mocking the creative strategies insurers devise for dodging claims is enjoyable, but insurers have a justifiable riposte: we customers can be equally creative with our application forms. Indeed, it's extraordinary how a congenital heart condition can slip the mind when ticking boxes and how dramatically our annual mileage shrinks on paper when we buy car insurance. Untruths and evasions will return to torment us if we do not expose our unlovely side on the paperwork at the outset. Possibly our admissions will disqualify us from that particular policy. Anything out of the usual – be it a lung tumour or a thatched roof – tends to frighten insurers, and some have not yet entered the world of equality. A woman wrote in to me after she became pregnant halfway through her annual travel insurance policy. Not only did the insurer inform her that she would now not qualify for medical expenses if she travelled abroad, but it refused to let her pay to extend her cover and declined to refund the cost of the outstanding months on her now worthless policy. Another reader discovered that quoted premiums for life insurance soared from £7 to £34 when he stated that he was gay, even though he was a keep-fit teetotaller in a long-term relationship.

Insurers, understandably, would like us to be identikit heterosexual thirty-somethings with a preference for Ford Escorts, post-war houses and sedentary holidays in unthreatening parts of Europe. Legally, they are entitled to infer that gay applicants are promiscuous AIDS sufferers and young men reckless drivers, although they should be able to show some evidence for their prejudices. However, they are not allowed to refuse cover on grounds of gender, disability, religion or sexuality. If they do so, report them to the FSA and take your custom elsewhere.

The secrets in the small print

Once you have signed up to a policy you should receive a schedule detailing your cover. This should arrive within a month. If it does not, demand it. Exhausted though you may be from your trawl through the terms and conditions, read it thoroughly. If it's holiday insurance make sure that the dates tally with your trip and that your daughter's diabetes is acknowledged and check in advance the procedures if you need to make a claim. Most policies will, for instance, require a crime reference number if you claim for theft, so if someone steals your camera you would need to contact the local police.

There may be times when it seems cheaper and easier for you to stump up rather than make a claim and pay the excess. Beware, though. You might be letting yourself in for more expense than you had bargained for, particularly if an injury is involved. Even though it may seem slight at the time, should long-term effects arise afterwards, the insurer will be unconcerned if you failed to alert them in the first place. Even if you do not wish to make a claim the terms and conditions of most policies require you to inform the insurer promptly about an incident so that you are covered later on should the need arise. You might be punished for your honesty, however. One reader assumed that no claims bonuses are a small reward for policy-holders who do not make a claim. When a cyclist rammed the side of his car he duly reported the incident to his insurer but paid for the damage himself. To his dismay his no claims bonus was reduced and his premiums were increased in case the cyclist decided to make a claim. This, unhappily, is common practice, although policy-holders should get their original premiums and bonuses reinstated and the difference refunded if no third-party claim arises within three years.

The computer says no

Now we get to the fun bit. One of the great amusements of my column has been observing the excuses insurers come up with to avoid paying their dues. Occasionally, customers provide them with all the justification they need. If you forget to alert them to a change in circumstances, if you underestimated the value of your car or overestimated the worth of your antique collection, if you failed to pay a couple of premiums or neglected to mention your troublesome hernia, you invalidate your claim all by yourself.

If, however, you abide by the small print the insurer will work out ways to disqualify your claim for you. It's important to remember that the insurance industry is deeply religious. Such is the awe that they have for the Almighty that they decline to intervene when He sees fit to smite your Peugeot or chimney stack or holiday timetable. These mishaps are reverently termed Acts of God, which usually apply to natural disasters and freak events that couldn't have been predicted or prevented by humankind. There was an occasion when God decided to launch a sheep from a mountainside on to the roof of a passing car. The car was wrecked, but because the insurance company blamed divine malice the driver had to buy a new vehicle out of her own funds.

At this point it's worth asking what insurance is for. Financial protection against unexpected mishaps would be the logical answer. After all, if a recurrence of a cancer or the submergence of a house built on a flood plain is to be expected, most insurers would refuse to cover you. Clearly an airborne sheep is unexpected. Nor can the blame be laid entirely at God's door, for if the farmer had fenced off the road and the sheep had taken better care the car would have sped by unmolested.

Another driver who wrote in would be a good deal richer if her neighbour's fence hadn't crashed on to her car. Said neighbour's insurers refused to pay out because the damage was unforeseen. 'Surely if events were foreseen we wouldn't need insurance,' wrote the unlucky car owner. Legally, the insurers were right. Sort of. A policy-holder is liable for damage inflicted on a third party only if it can be proved that they have been negligent. If the victim could have proved that the fence was so rickety that collapse was inevitable it would have counted as a foreseeable event and she would have been in possession of a shiny new car. But, the insurer argued, the fence was strong and beautifully nurtured and so it's demise could not have been predicted. Ordinary minds might wonder why, if it was so strong it caved in, but ordinary minds would have to wonder that expensively in court.

The moral of these tales is predictable and dull: always read the small print. There are policies out there that will cover freak events, but you need to know what kinds of mishaps are excluded. Obviously, if you live beside a river a flooded home is going to be less of a surprise than if you are perched halfway up a mountain, so you would need to be prepared. If the schedule murmurs indistinctly about Acts of God ring up and press your provider until you can be sure exactly what kind of events they have in mind.

The unpleasant truth about pay day

Now let us suppose that Sheep Lady and Fence Lady had submitted their claims successfully. Do not for one moment imagine that they will be bought a brand new Audi Q5 to replace their cherished vehicle. They will be given a cheque based on the market value of the car, and if it's more than three years old the pay-out might fund a third-hand Skoda. The market value will inevitably shock you. Insurers aren't interested in the fact that you installed shag pile carpets and waxed and polished weekly. They are not even interested in the used car prices on the forecourt of your local car dealer. Their bibles are one of two racy tomes – Glass's or Parker's guides – which calculate the basic value of a vehicle based on its age, make and mileage. For a small fee you can depress yourself by discovering how little your car is worth at www.glass.co.uk or www.parkers.co.uk.

Similarly, if your house burned to the ground your compensation would not allow you to cruise round John Lewis replacing your possessions (unless you are an MP); it would reflect the fact that your bed had seen you through your last two marriages and that you had already clocked up years of pleasure from your clothes, curtains and Le Creuset collection. Moreover, unless you had specified that your great-grandmother's diamond tiara was kept in the top bedroom you would receive no extra for lost valuables. If this matters, pay extra for an insurance policy that offers new for old in the event of loss or damage and, whatever cover you choose, always provide details of any significant items that may need extra protection.

How to flee a rip-off

It's an unfair fact that you provide an insurance company with a reliable income for ten years then, should you have to ask them for the protection you have paid for, they punish you by doubling your premiums. Exhausted though you may be after the tedious slog of selecting a policy, be wary of sinking into inertia, for the market is ever changing and you may miss out on far better deals. Companies often punish customer loyalty by hiking premiums year on year and using the profits to seduce newcomers with bargain deals. You could save yourself hundreds of pounds a year on your home or car policies if you shop around, and there are numerous price comparison websites to help you do that. General policies, bar one off-travel cover, tend to last for 12 months, but if you seek escape at the end of that time you need to be vigilant. Most insurers will renew a policy by default unless you find the energy to instruct them otherwise, and they rely on the fact that you are distracted by far more entertaining concerns to bother to do so.

Even if the effort of shopping around for an alternative is too much for you, you must take the trouble of reading your renewed schedule to check that the price and the cover are what you signed up to. One *Guardian* reader was pleased to discover that her automatically renewed credit card protection policy boasted higher levels of fraud protection and other superior treats. She was less delighted when she found that her premiums had been increased without warning or consent by 150 per cent to pay for these bonuses (this price hike had been omitted from the blurb). Her bank, which sold her the policy, explained that she had been elevated to the most expensive option within its new three-tier system because it believed that this best suited her needs.

This is the lovable thing about insurers. They do sincerely believe that they know what's best for their customers – and the fact that this best benefits their own coffers is mere coincidence. Another reader who took out a payment protection plan through his bank decided to cancel the policy and trust to a healthy future. The bank wrote back with descriptions of the diseases and disasters that could impoverish him, but the customer remained resolute. The bank, however, decided that he must be protected from his own folly and continued to help itself to premiums. Better this, though, than the insurer who promised a customer that his home contents insurance would be renewed automatically then forgot to renew it so that he spent half a year unknowingly without cover. Naturally, he should have checked his bank statements sooner and will, hopefully, do so from now on, mark each renewal date in his diary and raise a clamour if the replacement schedule doesn't come through. His saga boils down to the same crucial point: read those terms and conditions for information about renewing a policy, make sure insurers are kept up to date with your address so that you receive any reminders, and check that the correct premiums are flowing reliably from your bank account.

How to get your dues

Ideally, most of us will have little cause to test our insurers' sympathies. A good number of Britons have no idea what cover they shell out for year by year – that the £5 that vanishes monthly from their account protects a credit card that has long since been shredded. And hopefully, if and when we do make a claim, the insurer, after a decent show of reticence, will lob some cash our way. Premiums loyally paid are, however, no guarantee of compensation.

When a life assurance provider insists that your double hip replacement is no cause for early retirement you need to commence battle. Check first that the company is not, exasperatingly, in the right: that your claim is not excluded in the terms and conditions, that you have followed ordained procedures and that your payments are up to date. Once you have satisfied yourself that you are beyond reproach it's time to vent your ire on the insurer. Do this gracefully, restrainedly and in writing, spelling out the reasons why you feel your claim should have been honoured, and scoring a highlighter pen through any clauses in the policy that back you up. Names, addresses and preferred methods for complaints should be provided in the key facts sheet sent out when you bought the policy.

If, after the eight weeks that the regulators allow insurers to ponder laments, the response is unhelpful – or if you are unsure how to set about making the complaint – you can appeal for free to the Financial Ombudsman Service (www.financial-ombudsman. org.uk), which will contact the company on your behalf. You will need to fill out a complaints form and return it by post with your signature and copies of any relevant documents. This won't be a quick fix – the service aims to resolve complaints within six to nine months, although half are sorted by informal mediation after a few weeks. Should the adjudicator find in your favour it has powers to award you up to £100,000 at the expense of the insurer (alas such riches are rare), and although its decision is binding on the insurer it can't fine or punish the offender. Revenge might yet be yours, though, for if it considers your mistreatment has wider implications the ombudsman can confer with the FSA and the Office of Fair Trading, which do have powers to discipline miscreants.

If you disagree with the ombudsman's verdict you can still take your case to court, although brace yourself for hefty costs if you lose. The ombudsman reckons that it finds in favour of the customer in around a third of disputes, in favour of the company in another third and, in the last third, the company is deemed to be legally in the right but has confounded its customers with such gobbledygook that it's no surprise the latter was confused.

CHECKLIST

- Treat extended warranties and Payment Protection Insurance with caution. They are usually worth more to the retailer than to you. If you are tempted, don't accept a policy offered by a store until you have checked what policies are available elsewhere.
- Shop around when you are buying any kind of insurance. Don't look at price alone; there may be wide variations in cover.
- If you have any special requirements consult a broker who, for a fee or a commission, will be able to find you the most suitable plans.
- Make sure that your chosen insurer is registered with the Financial Services Authority.
- Be honest on the application forms about pre-existing medical conditions, floods, break-ins or any other unpleasantness. If you conceal anything your policy may be invalidated.
- Study the terms and conditions for any exclusions

or requirements that may affect you and ask for more information if anything is unclear.

- Make sure policy documents have arrived within the month whether you are taking out new insurance or renewing existing cover.
- Look out for cheaper deals shortly before your contract expires. Companies often penalise loyal customers by saddling them with higher premiums.
- Inform your insurer promptly of any incident, even if you do not intend to claim. A delay might invalidate any subsequent claim.
- If you are unhappy, follow the insurer's complaints procedure. If the issue is still not resolved the Financial Services Ombudsman offers a free mediation service.
- If you are dissatisfied with the ombudsman's decision you can still go to court.

6
Banks

Marianne Thomas is a student with little money, but she nonetheless makes several direct debit donations to charities. One day a £6 payment to Shelter was refused by her building society, Nationwide, because it would have left her account £1.02 in the red. For this sin Nationwide required a £131 penance. First came a £30 fine to compensate the building society for the effort of refusing the direct debit, then another £30 because the direct debit was re-presented and re-refused. Despite the fact that the building society had declined to grant her an overdraft of £1.02, it next levied a £20 charge plus interest for an 'unauthorised overdraft' of £1.02. Several days later the offending direct debit was once more presented and once more refused, and another £20 overdraft fee plus interest was deducted. Given that Thomas never did go overdrawn because the direct debit was never accepted, how, she wondered, could she be charged two different kinds of penalty for one 'offence'.

Thomas had a cashcard account, which, Nationwide explained, does not allow an overdraft facility, so even an overspend of 1p would incur vast charges. And the charges put the account even more into the red, so even more charges arose . . . and so on. It's what (if you were a bank) you might call a win-win situation.

A couple of years ago this might have been a short chapter. So mighty and invincible were our nation's banks in those happy times that their misdoings barely featured in my postbag. They may have been disciplining us with immoral penalty charges, doling out our savings to impostors and spinning complainants round unbreachable automated answer systems, but on the whole, provided an acceptable number of digits appeared on our statements, we were content. Now that we own the greater part of some of the biggest high street names we know better. All the while our money was funding manoeuvres so complex that even the bankers didn't understand them, and if it were not for the magnanimity of the taxpayer our personal fortunes would have evaporated along with those once respectable logos.

This is the big, scary picture. Down on the ground banking life proceeds pretty much as before, even if our accounts are emptier and loans are scarcer. However, the folly and fallibility of those who safeguard our money, exposed so terrifyingly in recent years, should make us more vigilant about which bank we choose and how it behaves towards us.

The automated answering maze and how to navigate it

There are few friendlier faces than a bank that craves

our custom, and few deafer ears than a bank that has done us wrong. Generally, if we pay in a four-figure sum each month, draw out a little less than that and keep our head down it will prove an amiable enough companion. All banks want, after all, is to spend our money in peace and to add a dainty amount of interest each month to show their goodwill. Customers can, however, prove tiresomely demanding. They move their money around and get annoyed if a few pounds are lost in transit. They overspend and object if the penalty fees exceed their debt. They allow their handbags to be stolen at bus shelters and dislike the discovery that their account has been emptied by a stranger. Worse, they want to ring up and complain about it.

Banks, it must be said, have a proper regard for the telephone when they are doing the dialling. Their friendly voices disrupt many a dinner party as they urge us to buy their home insurance or upgrade our credit cards. They do not, however, like to be interrupted by unsolicited calls from the public. Some while back, most banks and building societies did away with telephone numbers for their local branches and substituted a single, more expensive number. Where once customers might have included their local bank manager at their barbecue parties, now they are at the mercy of Del in a call centre in Sunderland. This strategy eliminated many calls, but not all, so then some banks decided to send customers on a telephonic tour of Southeast Asia. To prevent too many of them disturbing the call-centre staff there, they imposed automated menus that fed into more automated menus so that after five minutes of button stabbing the customer would be dumped in corporate finance, then cut off. All this can be an expensive pastime.

If it gets you nowhere select a free 0800 number from the customer contacts list (most banks have at least one – usually allocated to the sales department) and ask to be put through to the relevant section. The operative may jettison you mid-transfer, but if you do make it to your end destination you will have saved some pennies (unless you're using a mobile, but that's another story).

If you had the time and patience you would ring up different banks and building societies and test the efficiency of their answering systems before choosing where to deposit your money. You'd be able to gauge what lies in store only if you sampled the automated options available to existing customers however, for sales numbers aimed at newcomers are usually answered with misleading alacrity.

The asterixed interest rate and other unpleasant surprises

In reality, however, it is a winsome interest rate that decides us, after which banks rely on our natural inertia to stay put. Beware those winsome rates, especially when they are ornamented with asterixes. Squint more closely at the footnotes and you may find that they are being dangled at you for the briefest duration just to tempt you in. Once you have endured the transfer of all your direct debits and standing orders you are likely to find that the deal becomes less cosy. The bank has to tell you about any unpleasant changes to its terms and conditions two months in advance. You have the right to cancel your account without further ado unless your contract specifies a required notice period, but the upheaval of switching to a rival is so unnerving that few customers can face it. As always, therefore, you should keep hold of the slippery little leaflet in which banks conceal their terms and conditions as these might vary significantly from institution to institution. Here's where you discover what punishments will be levied if you exceed your overdraft limit or bounce a cheque, how long you can expect to wait if you complain and how much notice you must give to close an account. It is worth pouring an invigorating drink and ploughing through all this as soon as you get it, for it will spare you disagreeable surprises if you tumble into overdraft.

Until recently the behaviour of banks and building societies was guided by the Banking Code, a set of standards which, on paper at least, ensured that profit-making did not cloud banks' natural human sympathies. The trouble was that the code was voluntary and not all financial institutions were signed up to it. In November 2009, the code was replaced by the Payment Services Regulations, devised by the European Commission to harmonise banking practice in European Union countries. In the UK these new rules are overseen by the Financial Services Authority which has the power to take stern action if they are breached. Broadly speaking, they are fairly similar to the old Banking Code, but there are some new requirements which ought to make life more comfortable for customers. Banks and building societies must now give out more information about payment transactions, for instance. They must pay interest on transfers as soon as the money arrives in an account and they must give at least two month's warning before they cut interest rates. The biggest change, though, won't be enjoyed until 2012 when electronic payments must reach their destination one working day after they are made (until then they are allowed up to three).

How to save your money (from oblivion)

Two years ago the logical move, if you found a bank or building society that appealed to you, would have been to strew your loans and life savings around its various account options and get on with the more fulfilling business of spending. That was before the banking empire toppled and nearly collapsed. Now, should you rejoice in great wealth, you should be sure not to keep more than £50,000 in any one institution. That is the sum that is guaranteed under the Financial Services Compensation Scheme in the not so unlikely event that a bank or building society goes bust, but it covers you for only £50,000 (including interest accrued, so keep your capital a little below that sum) per company. If you had an array of accounts with any one bank you stand to lose anything over and above that limit.

The trouble is that you might not be aware that your fortune is in the control of a single name because so many mergers over the years have confused the blood line. Make sure, therefore, that you know whether that familiar ex-building society is, in fact, owned by one of the high street big boys and be careful not to put your funds in both.

With a bit of luck all you will have to do, once you've committed yourself, is read through the monthly statements and any important leaflets that come slithering out along with them. And read them you must, no matter how shaming it is to see your indulgences flaunted in black and white. It's amazing how many of those who write in to me have discovered – months too late – that direct debits are still funding cancelled gym membership or mobile phone contracts. Your chances of a refund recede with each passing week, whether your account is being emptied by fraud or error, so it's vital to query unexpected expenditure promptly.

It's a sorry fact that most of us will be a victim of fraud at some time or another. The circumstances might not be something obvious like a stolen wallet. A phishing email, purportedly from our bank, might have tricked us into revealing our account details to a cyber thief. Cloning devices on a cash point might replicate our card. Someone rooting round our recycling box might collect enough data to set up accounts in our name and at our expense. It could even be that a passer-by pocketed a credit card receipt that we abandoned on a restaurant table and used the details to fund mail order hi-fi. Evidently it's up to us to take basic precautions. We should never respond to unsolicited emails purportedly from our bank or log on to a bank's web pages through an email link. We should avoid sharing our life histories on Facebook to guard against identity fraud, shred personal documents before binning them and digest credit and debit card receipts along with the coffee and mints.

Legal comforts

If the worst does happen, our nest egg is theoretically protected. Provided we report questionable transactions promptly we are liable for only a maximum of £50 of our losses unless the bank can prove that we have been negligent. Negligence can mean anything from keeping a note of our PIN number in our wallet to failing to update security software before banking online. Until recently banks frequently shouted 'negligence' when customers disputed inconvenient sums, especially if the thief had used the customer's PIN number to make a withdrawal. However, the new Payment Services Regulations have smoothed the way for customers who fear they have been a victim of fraud. Whereas, under the old Banking Code, banks and building societies could demand evidence from the customer to prove that a withdrawal was unauthorised, the onus is now on the banks to prove that it was not fraudulent and the fact that a PIN was used is no longer deemed incontestable proof of negligence. And even if we had stuck our PIN number to the back of our bank card, we are still only liable for the first £50 if it was a credit card or, if our account was already overdrawn, up to its agreed limit before the fraud. This is because the Consumer Credit Act, that amiable law that protects us from our own folly, kicks in if a stolen card is used to obtain credit, and withdrawing money from an overdrawn account – or causing an account to go overdrawn by withdrawing money – counts as obtaining credit. Many banks don't realise this, and the few that do are coy about passing on the glad tidings to their customers. The new Payment Services Regulations are, like the old Banking Code, very clear that customers are liable to pay their own debts if they acted with 'gross negligence', but the Consumer Credit Act contradicts this when stolen cards are used as what it calls a 'credit token' and the Financial Ombudsman Service previously ruled that the act must take precedence over the old code. It found, therefore, in favour of a woman who had kept her credit card in a drawer along with a note of her PIN number and whose account was subsequently emptied by her son, even though her bank accused her of gross negligence.

Banks and building societies detest the Consumer Credit Act – and no wonder. It holds them jointly liable with the trader if the new bed you ordered sags in the middle or if the double-glazing firm you signed your

savings over to does a runner (provided you used a
credit card or credit agreement and spent between £100
and £30,000). The same organisations that are so
dogged about terms and conditions when a customer
steps out of line can be remarkably flexible when their
own coffers are threatened. Some years back
Barclaycard told a customer who had bought a faulty
leather bag that it could not help him because the shop
operated a no refunds policy. The customer persisted,
and Barclaycard, which had actually sent him a leaflet
explaining the Consumer Credit Act, replied helplessly
that since it was dependent on the goodwill of the
retailer it couldn't guarantee a successful outcome.
When the customer presented a written report from a
local trading standards official confirming that he was
entitled to a refund under the Consumer Credit Act,
Barclaycard tried a new tack and declared that the
trading standards authority was not a 'recognised
expert' and that its advice was invalid. It did eventually pay up to humour the *Guardian* and explained
that the confusion had arisen because of the 'grey area'
between the responsibility of the retailer and the point
where the credit card issuer assumes responsibility
(funny how such grey areas fade away when banks'
customers are deemed at fault).

There is, of course, no grey area. The Consumer
Credit Act is perfectly lucid about the fact that the
credit provider is 'jointly and severally liable' if a trader
is in breach of contract. If a card issuer refuses a valid
claim you can involve the Financial Ombudsman Service

or, if the disputed amount is not more than £5,000, you can threaten them with legal action quoting section 75 of the Act. They will probably settle before the case reaches the courtroom.

The curious cases of phantom funds

Matters get bloodier if the incompetent trader is our own bank. Most of us have long since ceased to expect any decent returns from our savings, but there is still one good reason to entrust them to a high street name rather than to the spare room mattress: security. If a thief makes off with the bags of notes in our bedroom we must resign ourselves to penury. If the same undesirable raids our bank account we can expect to get an equivalent sum restored to us. And because banks and building societies have complex security systems in place it should be a good deal more challenging for undesirables to reach our funds. These security systems are usually pretty effective, so much so that one reader who answered a security question wrongly found herself barred from her own bank account for two months.

These systems, however, do not prevent the banks themselves from losing our cash in the ether. Loud and numerous have been the laments from readers who have transferred money from one account to another and found that the sum never reached its destination. This may be because they mistyped the account number or that the money found its way to an excitingly named 'suspense account' – a temporary resting place for funds when there is a query about, or a problem with, its intended destination. Or it could be that the bank simply lost the paperwork. A pensioner who took a cheque for £1,155 into his NatWest branch to pay off his Alliance & Leicester credit card account found, when his statement arrived, that the money had never made it. Moreover, he was fined £50 for defaulting on his repayments. Natwest blamed Alliance & Leicester; Alliance & Leicester blamed Natwest. Alliance & Leicester did once manage to get to the phone and left a message saying that NatWest would not speak to it. When our pensioner rang back he was told the person who had left the message could not take calls from customers.

It's easy enough to prove that vanished sums once existed, provided you hang on to the receipts and remember to check them against your statement. If you did the transfer online you won't have a receipt, obviously, but your statement will show that the money left your account. It may be less simple to get anyone at the bank to take an interest in the disappearance, so rather than devoting the ensuing weeks to the telephone, write in with your grievance, enclosing copies of the receipt and copies of the denuded bank statement. If that fails to enrich your account, skip to the end of this chapter and involve the ombudsman.

The pensioner's experience reflects a wonderfully modern problem. In ancient days, when moving funds meant heaving sacks of gold about, people's fortune was a tangible entity. Today it is a row of flickering digits on a screen, and those digits can be illusory. Very definitely real, however, are the penalties imposed by banks when their cyber transactions are not as quick as they appear to be. One correspondent had received a £1,000 payment and, examining his account online, saw that the balance had indeed swelled by a grand. He therefore transferred the sum to his savings account, then discovered later that he had been charged three £25 penalties for three failed direct debit payments. It transpired that although the £1,000 payment had shown up on his account it had not actually been credited until the end of that day, after he had transferred the sum to his savings account. That transfer therefore plunged his account briefly into the red. Alliance & Leicester, for it was them again, refused to discuss this annoyance by telephone and insisted the charges were justified. They changed their minds, of course, when the *Guardian* came sniffing, but the fact remains that a healthy balance does not always signify healthy funds.

It is a curious technological perversity that while humans can tread moonrock, and emails can cross the globe in seconds, banks have traditionally required three or four days for credits to appear in accounts (building societies were allowed six). Even more curious is the fact that they possess the technology to debit the same accounts instantly. CHAPS payments are processed the same day, but you have to pay a hefty fee for such speed. BACS, the most usual form of online payment, currently take three days to inch their way from one account to another. In 2005 the Office of

Fair Trading (OFT) decided that such quaint processes should be hurried along a little to catch up with more enlightened parts of Europe. Three long years later the Faster Payments Service arrived. This marvellous advance allows funds to be transferred within two hours and most – but not all – high street organisations signed up to it. There is a downside: you still have to use BACS to shift funds over a certain threshold, and that threshold can vary from £10 to £10,000 depending on the bank (another reason to study those terms and conditions).

There's another problem: it doesn't always work. One reader defaulted on his mortgage payment and was fined £76 after he had used Lloyd's Faster Payment Service to transfer the necessary funds two days beforehand. The money should have cleared within hours; instead, it took four days. Lloyds argued that it warned customers that faster payments may take several days.

The new Payment Services Regulations have tried to address these problems and electronic money transfers should now reach their destination one working day after the payment is made, although until 2012 banks and building societies can allow themselves up to three working days. Cheques, though, are a different matter. These can take up to six days to clear, although you should start earning interest within two and can access the money within four (but if on day six the cheque bounces you're in a pickle).

The lesson here is obvious. Do not believe your

eyes. If your online account tells you that you are halfway to your first million postpone any spending frenzy for a day or two until you can be sure that the figures represent real money. Otherwise, your bank will spend your money for you – in vicious penalty charges.

The bankers' revenge: penalty charges and how to shrink them

Here we come to the most loudly detested banking vice. Slither one penny over your authorised overdraft and you are likely to be fined 6,000 times the sum, even if the bank's own incompetence tipped you over the threshold. Allow a cheque to bounce, and you'll have to pay double figures for the privilege of receiving a terse letter from the bank about it. And if you don't pay, the bank can place a default notice on your credit reference file, which will screw up your financial reputation for six years – ordinary mortals require a county court judgment before they can blacken a debtor's name on the credit register.

This skewed justice has long upset the Office of Fair Trading, which reckons that charges should reflect the actual costs involved in handling an unauthorised overdraft and not be punitive. In February 2009 it won the legal right to investigate whether penalty charges for overdrawn current accounts are unfair. The banks, naturally, are dismayed at the prospect of losing this limitless source of income, and so, having lost one appeal against the OFT, they are appealing to the Supreme Court to have the OFT's new powers overturned. At the time of going to press, the Supreme Court is still pondering the issue and so, in the meantime, the banking regulator the Financial Services Authority has put a hold on customer complaints about unfair fees. Don't let that put you off. You have six years in which to complain about an unfair charge, and this temporary moratorium won't count towards the deadline. Most banks have already set up their own charge refund departments, and some will consider reimbursements in individual cases. You may have to wait until the OFT has completed its report before you get a response, but at least your complaint will be recorded and you'll be nearer the front of the queue when things start moving again.

Credit card customers, equally martyred by penalty fees, are unaffected by the limbo and can have their grievances heard now. The OFT has already ruled that customers should not have to pay more than £12 for defaulting on their credit card payments, so if you have been charged more be constructively indignant with your card issuer.

Sadly, no one is saying that charges should be outlawed. When you open a bank account you are agreeing to a contract, and if you breach that contract by overspending then you will have to pay the price or face the courts. The point is, the price should reflect the cost to the bank. Anyone who has spent an afternoon with the Unfair Terms in Consumer Contracts

Regulations 1999 knows this. If the price of your ill-discipline is inflated it becomes a penalty charge, and no court can enforce this. So, on the next rainy Sunday, excavate the last six years of bank statements if you still have them. If you don't, write to the bank, cite the Data Protection Act and demand, politely, a list of what was charged when and why over that period. The bank has a legal duty to oblige you within 40 working days and is not allowed to charge more than £10 for the favour. This stinginess exasperates bankers, naturally, since they see enquiries about excessive fees as an opportunity to charge more excessive fees. The law takes no interest in what they charge for supplying old statements, so don't be surprised if your bank tells you it can't provide lists of charges – only back copies of statements in return for a large fee. The magic words Data Protection Act will shield you if this happens, because the Act forces them to obey you. If they still refuse, complain to the Information Commissioner at www.ico.gov.uk.

Your bank may require you to fill in a form, and it probably won't be in any hurry to get it to you, so ask about this in the letter and phone to chase if you don't hear anything within a week. When you've got the figures examine them. You might need a half-hour break to get over the shock; then apply logic. That letter informing you that you have exceeded your overdraft facility – did it really cost £25 to print a template off the computer and frank it? The most generous estimate would be £10. And given that, if a cheque bounces, the bank merely has to disgorge a pre-written letter to the other party – a £30 charge is sheer greed. Calculate just how much has been unreasonably wrested off you over the years and write requesting a refund under the Unfair Terms in Consumer Contracts Regulations 1999.

At the time of this book going to press, current account holders will probably have to wait for a response until the legal impasse between the banks and the OFT has been resolved, but if you are complaining about credit card fees you should set a time limit for the card issuer to respond – 14 days would be fair. If you hear nothing by the end of the fortnight write again and ring for good measure. Your card issuer may now attempt to wrong foot you by insisting that their charges are legitimate and that you have misinterpreted the law. You'll probably experience fleeting self-doubt, but banish it. The law could not be clearer on the matter, and you can threaten court action if they mess you around. If it gets this far – and usually by this stage banks will realise that you mean business and will settle outside the courtroom – it's a wise precaution to open a new bank account elsewhere and move any personal loans in case your foe turns nasty and disowns you. Solidarity in numbers is always consoling when matters reach a critical stage, so if you need moral support take a look at websites and forums dedicated to the subject such as www.consumeractiongroup.co.uk and www.which.co.uk, both of which offer templates for letters to reclaim fees.

Mortgage exit fees

Another healthy source of income that has bolstered bankers' pension pots are mortgage exit fees. You might not have noticed these malicious little stings in your mortgage contract – most people only register the threat of early repayment charges if they defect to another lender or pay off their loan before the contracted period has expired. But even if you have remained loyal to a single lender for 25 years you are still likely to have to pay a substantial sum to be released from their clutches when the loan period comes to an end. The Financial Services Authority reckons that these are too substantial. Banks and building societies claim that the charge compensates them for the bore of releasing the deeds and notifying the Land Registry, but, as with penalty charges, the fees should reflect the actual costs incurred by the company – probably around £50 rather than the £200 levied by some companies. If the sum comes to more than the figure in the contract – and it often does, because exit fees have soared in the last few years – complain, unless the bank can point to increased costs to justify it. You should demand back the difference between the fee enshrined in your contract and the inflated sum that they have charged you.

Where to turn for rescue

If your bank refuses to cooperate on fee shrinkage or any other issue complain to the Financial Ombudsman

Service (www.financialombudsman.org.uk/consumer/ complaints.htm). This benevolent authority will listen for free to woes arising from all banking matters as long as you have given the offending party a chance to resolve the issue. When you feel that your bank or building society has wronged you and a visit to your local branch or a telephone call fails to soothe you, find out about that company's official complaints procedure and follow it. This will typically involve writing or speaking to the department responsible for the problem or to your branch manager. Then, if you have not received a satisfactory response within a set time – anything from five days to four weeks, depending on the company – you would send a letter to the dedicated complaints department. You'll find information on this by keying 'complaints' into the search box on the bank's website. To speed things up remember to include obvious details that people so often omit, such as your account number, address and telephone number. Write 'Complaint' at the top of the letter, clip on copies of any relevant paperwork and state clearly and briefly what has gone wrong and what you wish done to put it right. If the bank has breached the Payment Services Regulations (whiz through the code quickly the night before to find out) mention it – it shows that you are aware of your rights and cannot easily be fobbed off.

Whether you phone or write (and writing is a good idea because it leaves a paper trail) keep a log of names and dates. The Financial Services Authority obliges banks to reply within eight weeks. If, after this time, you haven't had a satisfactory reply or a reply at all, or if, before the eight weeks is up, the bank declares it can't or won't help, you are free to contact the ombudsman. Do it while your blood is up because if you delay more than six months after the eight-week deadline (or after the bank washes its hands of your grievance) the service won't be able to help you. Bear in mind too that if you pursue your foe through the courts first you can't then turn to the ombudsman. You can, however, take the legal route if the ombudsman can't resolve the problem to your satisfaction. You'll have to cultivate unusual restraint, for the ombudsman can take up to nine months to investigate a tricky case, although half are sorted within weeks.

CHECKLIST

- Read the terms and conditions to check, for instance, what fees are charged and when.
- If a bank alters any of its terms and conditions you can cancel your account without notice within 60 days of being informed.
- Never keep more than £50,000 in any one institution or its subsidiaries so that all savings are protected by the Financial Services Compensation Scheme.
- Always read your statements and query any inexplicable payments immediately.
- If money is stolen from your account you are liable only for a maximum of £50, unless you have been negligent with your bank details. If your account

was overdrawn when the fraud took place your liability is still £50, even if you had been negligent.

- Make sure that money really is in your account before making payments or transfers. Some credits can show up on screen before they have arrived in your account.
- If things go wrong follow the complaints procedure of the bank or building society. If there's no satisfactory response after eight weeks involve the Financial Ombudsman Service.

7
Utilities

Once upon a time there was a single mother who struggled to raise four young sons on benefits. Along came a wicked giant who desired her income for himself, and so he diverted it into his own pocket. When she tried to flee, he held her captive so that he might continue to add her money to his huge piles of gold. And so he became richer and she became poorer, and there was nothing that anyone could do about it.

Janine Stewart was the mother; British Gas was the ogre. The story began when she moved in to her Cambridge council house, and because money was tight, Stewart asked British Gas to install card meters to control her gas and electricity supplies. A few weeks later she got a bill for £900. And so began a string of phone calls to persuade British Gas to admit its mistake. Far from confessing, however, the company said it would dock £5 every time she inserted her meter card until the debt was cleared.

And so it did. Desperate, Stewart tried to escape to a different supplier, but British Gas refused to release her until she paid the mysterious debt and continued to dock £5. A year later, it tired of the game and acknowledged that the bill was probably due to an incorrect meter reading when her gadget was installed, but then the company lapsed into silence. Seven months on, a neighbour took up her cause and was told by British Gas that it was company policy to help itself to customers' money before it had been proved that they owed anything. It would, it said, begin an investigation, but it would be another 28 days before it decided whether Stewart was due to get back the money it had docked from her.

Life is conceivable without banks, it would probably be improved without planes, and we could doubtless build a fulfilled existence without the input of insurers. Utilities companies, however, are a different matter. They warm us and water us and deliver to us episodes of *Desperate Housewives*. We ought to venerate them. Perhaps, though, it is because we are so slavishly dependent on them that we loathe them with such vigour. When the government surveyed consumer confidence in 45 different sectors, energy was ranked bottom.

At least since 1998, when the industry was privatised, we have been free to pick and choose whom we start a relationship with, but that very choice is unnerving given the questionable charms of the candidates. And once we have mustered the stamina to shift suppliers we may briefly enjoy diminished bills, but the chances are that the service will remain dispiritingly similar. A survey conducted by the Citizens Advice Bureau in 2008 found that a third of customers had been left hanging on the end of the line for more that 30 minutes when they called their supplier and a quarter were dissatisfied with the way their call had been handled. It's the usual story. There is no zeal equal to that of a supplier who craves your custom. So embracing is their energy, indeed, that fresh-faced missionaries are liable to arrive on your doorstep, haul you away from your children's bath time and perform frantic feats of arithmetic to demonstrate how much richer they could make you if you would autograph their clipboard. Obviously such attentions are flattering and obviously you feel tempted to oblige them to prevent those fresh faces from clouding (or just to dislodge them from your pathway).

And certainly, to start with, the vigour continues in the most promising manner. Celebratory missives will pour forth from this new supplier welcoming you into your new corporate family. Sorrowful missives will pour forth from your old supplier mourning your defection. You might even start to save some money. But, when you discover that you are being billed for the energy consumption of the small supermarket down the road, the zeal will evaporate. The fresh faces give way to automated voices and computer-generated platitudes and a succession of robotic Mels and Sues and Andys, who will promise call-backs that never come.

How to find a fulfilling relationship – and save money

Most of us, if we do once summon the energy to switch suppliers, are so exhausted by the adventure that we then stay put. A significant minority has hunkered down since the days of the gas and electricity boards and been effortlessly absorbed by British Gas. It is, however, our public duty to shimmy our way through the whole line-up of energy companies, for the premise behind privatisation is that customers will vote with their feet. If a supplier skimps on its customer services it will lose customers and will be inspired to reform. If, however, the customers are unhappy but inert the company will grow fat and smug and see no reason to invest its profits in pampering them. There's another even stronger reason for agility: gas prices have risen by 130 per cent since 2003, and electricity prices by 100 per cent. All of the companies are at it, but some more so than others, and a household can save itself several hundred pounds a year by seeking out a better deal. It may be a temporary bargain, for suppliers are like sheep – when one hikes its tariffs the others usually follow pretty close behind – but even so, it should be possible to find a supplier who can warm and illuminate you for less than its rivals. If you have time and tenacity you can do the sleuthing yourself, but it can be a bewildering process because each company offers a variety of different tariffs, in addition to which some levy a daily standing charge on top of the fuel price, others appear not to, but instead absorb the charge into their unit prices, and some exclude VAT (currently 5 per cent for fuel) from their quotes.

The easiest way to sniff them out is to key your details into a price comparison website. There is a dizzying multitude to choose from, but you can narrow it down to a dozen by making sure that your selection is signed up to the Confidence Code drawn up by the statutory campaigning body Consumer Focus. The website will pocket a small fee – between £30 and £60 – in commission each time they sign a new customer up to a supplier, but the code requires them, among other things, to be independent and impartial. You can find a list of accredited services on the Consumer Focus website at www.consumerfocus.org.uk.

Resisting sales seductions

The trouble with price comparison websites from a supplier's point of view is that they might steer customers into the arms of a rival. Hence those eager salesmen mentioned earlier. It is very rarely a good idea to give way to one of these, no matter how disarmingly they fling figures at you. Seldom do they agree to leave you with leaflets to study at your leisure. Often they do not even admit that they are touting for your custom. Instead they will inform you that their records show that you are paying too much for your gas or electricity, that they are, in fact, already your suppliers and that you are simply lining the pockets of a middleman. Then they will ask to examine your latest energy bills, which ought, of course, to be unnecessary since they have already claimed to know how much you are paying.

At this point you should bid them a polite farewell. If their spiel sounds inviting ask them to leave some paperwork so that you can examine their proposals at leisure once you have worked out for yourself how much you already spend. Do not touch their proffered ball-point pen, even if they beg you to sign to prove that they have visited you or sing of unbeatable bargains available that day only, and never ever hand over direct debit details to 'speed things up' should you transfer later on. If you do succumb, the salesperson must make sure that you have understood the contract and have explained your cancellation rights – the Doorstep Selling Regulations allow you seven working days in which to change your mind – before you sign. They should then leave you with a copy of the contract. You get the same seven days if you accept a telephone proposal during a telephone call. If they don't do any of this, or if they are loath to leave when you ask them to, you should report them to the government-funded advice body Consumer Direct (www.consumerdirect.org.uk).

The surreal world of Erroneous Transfers

Alas, even the grittiest resistance might not protect you from an unwelcome welcome pack in the post a few days later. In 1998 privatisation gave birth to a shadowy new breed of beings – the Erroneous Transfer (ET). These unfortunates are kidnapped either by accident or design from their chosen supplier and re-established with a rival. The explanation may be innocent – someone confused your meter reference number with your neighbour's and you were borne off to their intended supplier – or it could be more sinister – a salesperson who cold-called you might have tricked a signature out of you or forged it to boost their commission.

Occasionally ETs are dangled in a limbo, wrenched from their old supplier and transferred to destinations unknown. One Powergen customer discovered one day that she didn't officially exist. When she called to cancel her dual fuel account she was told that she had transferred to a new supplier two years ago and only this mystery new supplier could do the cancelling. This was doubly odd because she had never transferred her supply, and she had, over those two years, consistently received and paid bills to Powergen. Detective work identified Calortex as her new supplier, but Calortex denied all knowledge of her and insisted that her address did not exist. Powergen was unmoved by this difficulty and continued to insist that her new supplier must cancel her unwanted account. It turned out that when her neighbouring flat dweller had switched to Calortex her meter reference number had been recorded against her neighbour's address and her own home eliminated from official records.

It's bad enough to be the victim of one unfeeling monolith. Erroneous Transfers are stranded between two of them, and it's well known that energy companies hate talking to each other almost as much as they hate talking to wronged customers. Given that they are continually stalking, wooing and then jilting each other's customers this is understandable, but so paralysing is their hostility that the industry was prodded by the regulator Ofgem into drawing up the Erroneous Transfer Customer Charter to encourage them to communicate. This Charter states what should have been obvious all along: that customers whose accounts have been whisked off without their consent can contact either their old supplier or their unwanted new one to get themselves rescued and that both parties must liaise with each other. Whichever one they approach must explain when they can expect to be returned to their original choice, how their billing will be managed in the meantime and how the mistake happened. They are obliged then to dispatch a letter summarising all this within five days and another letter within 20 days, confirming that the customer will be transferred back. The unhappy ET should not receive any bills from their kidnapper during their captivity because their original supplier will still be responsible for the charges. This is wonderfully reassuring. The trouble is that the principles enshrined in the Charter are only targets. Ofgem takes a look every few years to see whether the companies are taking any notice of them, but customers are not entitled to statutory compensation if they decide it's all too much trouble. Nor can ETs demand compensation for their ordeal, although some companies will pay out a goodwill sum. If, however, a forged signature precipitated the adventure the victim can claim up to £250, provided that the offender is signed up to the Energysure code of practice, which sets standards for door-to-door sales.

Sorting saints from sinners

This code and others like it are worth bearing in mind when you are choosing a supplier. Tempting as it may be to leap into the arms of the cheapest candidate, you should skim through their policies first, for these can vary from company to company as widely as prices, and the terms can really matter when things go wrong. They will determine, for instance, how much grace you have before you are disconnected for non-payment, how often your meter will be read and how complaints are handled. The Big Six companies – British Gas, Scottish Power, Npower, EDF, E.on and Scottish and Southern – which between them supply 98 per cent of gas and electricity to British households, have formed the Energy Retail Association and have agreed on certain strategies to soothe distressed customers. You might still require three days' leave to get through to their customer services, but at least these pledges show that they are thinking kindly of you.

Take billing, for instance. It's difficult to judge whether I've heard more from customers trying to stem a turbulent tide of the things or from customers trying to coax just a single invoice from an implacable supplier. Powergen once turned an elderly widow living in sheltered accommodation into a corporate fat cat by transferring her account on to a pricey business tariff and cold-calling her to offer her office perks. Her complaints were ignored until the *Guardian* got involved, whereupon the company found that during a system upgrade her customer number had been mistyped and she had been transformed into a small business. It is truly frightening how much our wealth, health and sanity depend on these strings of digits and on the concentration of the person required to type them in.

Similar corporate butterfingers caused another woman to spend months pleading with her new supplier, Atlantic Electric and Gas, to send her a bill. Eventually, in despair, she returned to her old supplier and later received a huge bill from Atlantic for energy consumed in the weeks after she had left them.

Bills: the unsolved mystery

Most of the complaints about energy companies boil down to bills: inflated bills, incomprehensible bills, bills addressed to total strangers, bills for energy you have never used and from companies you have never heard of. It's extraordinary, therefore, that it was not until 2005, seven years after privatisation, that the Energy Retail Association came up with the Code of Practice for Accurate Bills. Even more extraordinary is the fact that only the six biggest companies are signed up to it. The most reassuring provision is that you do not have to pay more than one year's worth of debts if the supplier neglects to send you a bill for more than 12 months. It also requires companies to read customers' meters at least once every two years. Independent auditors check that the member companies are complying with the code, and the association promises to impose sanctions if they are not.

Checking your own meter is one of life's less engaging pastimes. Usually it involves perilous acrobatics around the ironing board in the understairs cupboard, but check it you must – preferably every time you get a bill – for the estimates that companies have to rely on otherwise can become wildly fanciful. And in the less likely event that their guesses are too low you will have to muster a sudden lump sum to pay off the balance. If you settle your dues by direct debit you will pay a set amount each month. In summer you will probably find your account awash with a surplus, the idea being that this will be absorbed in winter when you turn on the central heating. However, it's a canny trick of companies to set direct debits too high and then wallow in the extra cash. A Which? survey in 2008 found that one in five customers who had overpaid were in credit by more than £100, which means that an unwarranted £660 million are sloshing around industry coffers.

Any credit will be noted somewhere on the bill, often identified merely by the letters CR. Companies don't want you to notice this, of course, and if you cancel an account they often forget to mention that they owe you, so make sure you keep an eye on your bills and demand back any overpayments. This task can be amusing. One reader who was owed £900 by her supplier TXU spent seven months trying to wrest the sum back. TXU told me that she had not been refunded because 'she was owed so much'. 'Only about five people in the company are allowed to authorise payments over £200,' explained an official. At the same time the same company had withheld £120 in overpayments that it owed to a pensioner because, as it informed me, it had 'inherited computer systems that don't automatically send refunds', although its debit facility was so efficient it helped itself to payments long after the pensioner had cancelled his account.

There may come a time when the bills are punctual, lucid and accurate, but you cannot afford to pay them. Once you have explained this to the company – and you must explain as soon as the bill arrives, don't just hope that the demands will melt away – they should come up with a staggered payment plan that you can afford, or offer to install a pre-payment meter so that you can budget more efficiently. They cannot terrify you with a disconnection notice until at least 28 days after sending the bill, and this notice must give you seven days' warning. If you are threatened with disconnection and can't talk the company round, get in touch with Consumer Direct, which will probably ask Consumer Focus to intervene. In the case of emergencies such as this, the consumer team aims to resolve the issue within the next working day.

The above battles should be far less bloody if you check the reputation of a company whose cheap deals tempt you. Ofgem is to start publishing a breakdown of complaints received, and some comparison websites have used this information plus details of fines or misbehaviour imposed by Ofgem to rate the customer services of each company. If the best prices are offered by a company with poorly rated back-up you should think hard about whether the saving is worth it.

How to avenge corporate neglect

The codes of practice governing billing and doorstep selling that are meant to shield customers from scalliwaggery are voluntary, and smaller gas and electricity companies are not bound by them. However, there is compulsory redress for shoddy service, which suppliers would rather you didn't know about. The Gas and Electricity (Standards of Performance) Regulations 2005 are your saviour when you take the afternoon off work and wait in for a meter reader who never comes, or if you cannot persuade your supplier to fix an appointment, the regulations allow you £20 for your trouble. If your electricity supply is interrupted by planned works without at least two days' notice you pocket another £20, and if disrupted supplies are not restored within 18 hours (24 hours or more if severe weather cut you off), you are entitled to £50 plus an extra £25 for each subsequent 12 hours. Engineers must be dispatched to investigate issues with voltage or misbehaving meters within seven days, or else a letter should be sent diagnosing the problem within five days (£20 for you if they don't), and a failed fuse should be attended to within 3 hours on weekdays (£20 if not).

You are even entitled to £20 if a query about your electricity bill is not resolved within five working days – but only if you are signed up to one of the main regional suppliers. Moreover, these payments must reach you within 10 working days, otherwise £10 is added to the total. Customer services staff don't tend to know of this statutory bounty (funny that) and even fewer customers are aware of it, with the result that hardly anyone ever claims. If they did, the expense of pacifying them would doubtless persuade companies to invest more in pampering us all. Next time you are mistreated, therefore, check the Acts (you can find more readily digestible summaries on the Ofgem and Consumer Focus websites) and claim your few pounds for the sake of the common good.

When all else fails . . .

Each gas and electricity supplier will have their own complaints procedure, and, unfortunately, if something goes awry, you will have to battle your way through this first. Consumer Direct will advise on how to compile and direct your moan if you need back-up and will recommend what steps you should take next if you don't get the response you wanted. It's essential that, from the first time you pick up a pen or the telephone, you keep a log of dates and contacts, because timings can make or break your chances of redress, as you will see.

If the company doesn't reply within eight weeks (if you are with one of the Big Six, that is, because smaller companies that joined the new ombudsman scheme after 1 October 2008 have a luxurious 12 weeks to mull over your woe), or if it sends you a 'letter of deadlock' declaring that you are a fool and they intend to ignore you, you can involve the Energy Ombudsman. It wasn't until 1 October 2008 that it became mandatory for companies to sign up to this or any other approved redress service, and some didn't get round to it until 2009, so you need to find out whether your supplier is a member and when it joined before lodging a complaint (there's a list of members and their joining dates at www.energyombudsman.org.uk). If your grievance predates their membership the Ombudsman may not be able to help you, and generally the Ombudsman can't look into any problem with any company that happened before July 2006, although it can use its discretion if it deems a complaint worthy enough. Don't dawdle too long either, because you have to refer your problem within nine months of first raising it with the supplier. The Ombudsman has the power to award up to £5,000 as a goodwill gesture in certain circumstances, although the sin would have to have been pretty severe to win you even three figures – the average award for 2008–9 was £120.

Water

Because water companies often send bills only once or twice a year and because water tends to course nicely from our taps whenever we turn them on, most of us rarely give our suppliers a thought, unless a heatwave and untended leaks deprive us of the use of our hose. Even if we did have cause to notice them we couldn't end an unfulfilling relationship, because although the water industry has been privatised, we are all stuck with our specific regional supplier. Prices are regulated by the government watchdog Ofwat, and, because our enforced captivity with one supplier means that there is no incentive to study their prices and shop around, many of us probably have no idea what we pay for water and sewerage. It may be only when we are charged spectacularly absurd sums that we realise something is amiss.

There was the case of the church threatened with bailiffs because Thames Water reckoned that the vicarage was consuming enough water to irrigate a London borough. It took three years and press intervention to reveal that the company had miscalculated the bills, and water companies are as liable as their gas and electricity counterparts to confuse meter references and charge us for filling our neighbour's swimming pool. Come to think of it, I've heard from half a dozen single flat dwellers who have been charged several thousand pounds for running the odd bath and a dishwasher. So perhaps we ought to look at those annual demands with a little more interest.

To meter or not to meter?

Water companies can base their sums on a number of methods. Quaintly, the rateable value of your home is the most common, even though rates were abolished in 1990. The water charge is calculated in pence per pound of the estimated annual rental value, despite the fact that rateable values of private homes were last assessed between 1973 and 1990 and no one – not the government's Valuation Office nor the water companies themselves – can amend them. Nostalgics will appreciate this tie with the past, but it will do you no favours if you rejoice in a large manor, yet live in solitude and shower once weekly. On the other hand, water companies might charge a flat rate, regardless of the size of your property or your water consumption (happy tidings for populous families). Some companies band homes according to the size and the number of occupants and charge accordingly, or they use a water meter to record your precise consumption and bill you for that (the better option if you live austerely alone).

It's worth knowing how you are charged because you may be able to change it, although usually the choice is between a meter and only one of the above methods. Everyone is entitled to have a meter installed for free, unless you live in Scotland or it would be impractical or prohibitively expensive to do it. It could save you a couple of hundred pounds a year, although you must submit to the bore of waiting in for a meter reader, but if the resulting bills shock you you should be able to return to your old bad ways within 12 months. So far, companies can't force you to accept a meter, unless there are declared water shortages in your area or you waste profligate amounts on power showers or garden sprinklers.

Water, unlike gas or electricity, is deemed a human right, and so water providers cannot disconnect customers who can't or won't pay their bills. Instead, they have to take the legal route and obtain a county court judgment to get their dues. Your local Citizens Advice Bureau (www.citizensadvice.org.uk) will be able to help if you run into arrears, and you maybe entitled to help with payments if you have certain medical conditions or if you are on benefits with three children under 16 years of age.

The inescapable embrace and how to make the best of it

Exasperatingly, as I've said, if your water company offends you you can't seek sanctuary in the bosom of a more benevolent supplier. This is, of course, a mighty consolation for the regional giants that dangle us for half a day on their telephone helplines without fear of losing our custom. We can, however, menace them in a small-scale way by memorising the Guaranteed Standards Scheme, which forms part of the 1991 Water Industry Act (Scotland is covered by similar rules, but Northern Ireland so far has none).

This legislation anticipates the sufferings we may have to endure if we ever have to contact one of these monoliths, and it requires water companies to perform certain obvious functions, such as answering queries when we raise them, turning up for appointments within the promised time slot (companies must give you a two-hour slot rather than a morning or afternoon estimate if requested) and swabbing flooded sewage. Naturally, the companies don't always perform these functions, and often they get away with it because their customers have no idea that they are entitled to compensation if they don't.

One Thames Water customer begged the *Guardian* for mercy after her bathroom taps ran dry. She had needed a new supply pipe to her home, and the company had demanded that she pay £900 up-front to fund it. The sum was presumably to impress its accountants, for it did nothing in return for the money for seven months save to dig a large hole outside, which filled with water and flooded her basement. In the long meantime, the water pressure in her house ran so low that not a drop reached the first-floor bathroom. Interestingly, the company told me that it needs to sit on customers' cash from the outset of any planned works because it would otherwise have to fund jobs by financing agreements and would then need to raise connection charges. Another customer gained an unusual water feature – a stream of raw sewage across her front garden – and spent two months leaping over it before the *Guardian* nudged Thames Water into action.

It's a very small comfort, but the Guaranteed Standards Scheme would have entitled the first victim to £25 – statutory compensation if water pressure falls below a certain level twice in 28 days – and the second could have expected a refund of half her annual sewerage charge if the leak had 'materially affected' her property. Both should then have received £20 because their written complaints were not acted upon – you get the same sum if you don't get a timely reply to an account query plus a further £10 if these payments are late. They didn't, of course, because if the sum is not awarded automatically, customers have to claim it themselves in writing within three months, and because customer services staff tend to forget to mention their entitlements, very few customers know anything about them.

If you know anyone who has pocketed any of these sums you are rare. I certainly don't. If you feel that you are entitled to a statutory token of remorse write and tell the company so, spelling out your rights under the Guaranteed Standards Scheme. You can mug up on these at leisure on the website of the water regulator Ofwat (www.ofwat.gov.uk). If the company doesn't respond to this or any other issue, embark on the company's official complaints process, which will be described on the back of your bill and on their website. When all efforts in that direction fail, you can write to the Consumer Council for Water (www.ccwater.org.uk), and it should take up your grievance. Bear in mind that you're in populous company. Complaints to the council are surging each year, and most are about bills and charging, but even so most are resolved between 20 and 40 days.

CHECKLIST

- Never sign up with a doorstep salesperson until you have had a chance to read and digest their figures.
- The best way to find a cheaper gas or electricity supplier is to use a price comparison website. Make sure the one you choose is accredited to the Consumer Focus Confidence Code.
- Compare customer service ratings of different companies on the Consumer Focus website before you switch. A cheap deal coupled with poor back-up may seem less desirable than you at first thought.
- If you don't know who your supplier is you can call the Meter Point Number helpline on 0870 608 1524. Or find out who your regional distributor is (www.consumerfocus.org.uk publishes a list) and get them to tell you.
- Check your meter readings each time a bill arrives and note how much credit you have on your account so you can claim back any surplus.
- The Gas and Electricity Standards of Performance Regulations allow you statutory compensation if suppliers breach certain commitments. You can find these at www.consumerfocus.org
- If your supplier fails to resolve a complaint within 8 to 12 weeks contact the Energy Ombudsman at www.energyombudsman.org.uk
- Find out how your water bill is calculated. It may be cheaper to request another method or to have a meter installed.

- The Guaranteed Standards Scheme awards statutory compensation for poor service. These are outlined on the water regulator's website (www.ofwat.gov.uk).
- If a water company fails to resolve a problem you can complain to the Consumer Council for Water (www.ccwater.org.uk)

8

Telecoms

Anthony Kesten was a blameless resident of Milton Keynes who had a mobile phone account with O2. Suddenly, O2 decided that he could be improved upon and, without warning or reason, changed his name to Alan Kesten. As far as Kesten knew, there is no Alan Kesten in the whole of the UK, let alone in Milton Keynes, but this fact was of no interest to O2.

When he emailed the company to point out the mistake, he received standard replies that ignored his identity crisis, and when he asked for a call-back he was told that no one could speak to him because, being obstinately an Anthony, he was not the named account holder. Stalemate. Yet it took O2's press office a couple of hours to discover that Kesten's name was altered by a staff member when his phone was upgraded and to restore his original identity.

The basic concept behind the telecommunications industry is to enable humans to communicate. It's a comical fact, therefore, that communication is a skill that eludes the average telecoms company. It might take us, as customers, some time to realise this, for there are times when we prod a number into a telephone and someone at the other end answers (provided that our landline has not been inadvertently cut, our account mysteriously closed, our phone number donated to a neighbouring stranger or our upgraded mobile handset eviscerated by a previous owner). The chances, however, of that answering voice belonging to a telecoms customer services operative are remote, for telecoms companies, like their utility brothers, discourage verbal relationships with the public.

Complaints about telecoms could have fuelled the 'Dear Anna' column all by themselves over the decade. Admittedly, the technology has been evolving, sometimes painfully, all that while, and customer services have had to evolve (even more painfully) to keep up with it. When I began, Local Loop Unbundling, 3G phones and unmetered internet access were infant exotica; since then they have propelled us into a glorious new millennium, but at some cost to our mental equilibrium.

As usual, it was not so much the technical hiccups that tormented us, but the hours spent tolerating excerpts from *Peer Gynt* in queuing systems while we tried to tell someone about them.

Landlines

In the old days the only thing we had to worry about was our telephone landline. Remember those quaint devices tethered by flexes to the wall? Back then some of us were even still renting our handset from British

Telecom (check your bill; if you never notified them that you'd swapped it for a plastic talking hamburger you may still be paying a rental fee). Landlines, therefore, are a good place to start this chapter.

The chances are, if you still have one, that you are signed up to British Telecom. Large numbers of us, unless seduced by a rival's broadband and telephone package, have never bothered to sniff out the alternatives. If nothing has ever gone wrong with the service you are probably content with your old friend. It's when there is a problem that you find that one thing has remained constant over the years of flux: the near impossibility of getting through to an empathetic human. First, you might spend an hour in the automated wilderness that is customer services. That is just to get flesh and blood to greet you. When they do, you are likely to be told that you need a different department, and the transfer will fill up another half hour. This process may be repeated for a further hour, after which, if you are unlucky, you will be cut off. If fortune smiles, however, you will be promised a call-back. Don't count on it happening.

Undaunted by the fact that it can't listen to the customers it's got, BT has been expensively boasting of how many thousands have returned, scarred, to its fold, lured, in part, by its bargain deals. Life may indeed be cheaper for those who return – but that could well be because they will spend weeks without a telephone line. Three months is the time it took three readers to be reunited with the outside world after they signed over. A pensioner and his disabled wife were left incommunicado with relatives for four weeks because their number was changed without warning when they rejoined BT.

Then there was the case of the newly bereaved widow who asked to have her account transferred from her late partner's name to her own. Her line was terminated, her broadband account cancelled, and her long-held telephone number allocated to strangers. In the midst of funeral arrangements she was left without her telephonic lifeline. BT did eventually restore her old number, but only after sending a letter and two bills to her late partner, asking him to act as his own executor and assuring him that it wanted to make things 'as easy as possible at this difficult time'.

These dramas are by no means limited to BT. As companies slash their prices and swallow smaller competitors to grab custom, there is less money around to spend on frills. And frills, in the eyes of big business, include a direct line to a living being who is sufficiently paid, trained and supported to resolve individual concerns of customers. Computer technology is a far cheaper form of customer care, but computers, alas, are not known for their empathy with widows. Once an over-stressed call-centre operative mistypes a command – or blunders through a problem that defies decreed categories – the System takes over with an automated ruthlessness that ordinary mortals appear powerless to override.

Matters are not helped by the tortured processes required to achieve simple aims. One reader whose line was cut off unexpectedly spent days being whirled around BT's automated telephone system. He asked to lodge an official complaint but was told that he could complain only once an in-house complaints procedure had been initiated and that the complaints department only dealt with mishandled complaints. To initiate the in-house complaints procedure he had to return to the automated answer maze.

When you have a problem with a telephone line or when you want a new line installed you fall into the hands of Openreach, regardless of who supplies your telephone service. Openreach, which just happens to be owned by BT, was set up to ensure that rival telephone companies get equal access to BT's own local network – that is, the wiring that connects each household to the local telephone exchange. It calls itself the 'proud guardians of BT's local access network' and is responsible for maintaining all the wires and fibres that link customers with the network of their chosen provider. The trouble is that householders can't contact Openreach directly. If the promised technician doesn't turn up, they have to complain to their provider, which will, if they get round to it, alert Openreach and then, possibly, within the ensuing few days get back to said householder with an update. If the provider doesn't get round to it you're stuck because Openreach will not deal with individuals.

One reader, noticing an Openreach technician up a pole outside her house, discovered that he was fixing a fault on her neighbour's line. She tested her own line, found it dead and asked if the man could fix hers too while he was up there. He refused because she hadn't reported the fault to her provider, and so she had to call a helpline and wait in for three days for another technician, who didn't turn up.

How to find a telecommunications company that telecommunicates

Telecoms companies can get away with all this because none of the authorities take stock of their overall performance. The telecommunications regulator Ofcom sees no reason to print an annual audit of complaints for the public to scan before choosing a provider because, it argues, complaints are hard to validate and customers can transfer to another company if they are unhappy. However, it has asked some fixed-line service providers to publish limited information about their quality of service. The result is the website www.topcomm.org.uk, which compares billing accuracy, how quickly complaints are resolved, reported faults and service provision of 12 companies. Unfortunately, this does not, as yet, cover mobile phone or internet service providers. There are numerous comparison websites to help you find a good deal, but these focus on the cheapest price, not the most reliable service. Uswitch.com is the exception – it prints an overall score plus a breakdown of strengths and weaknesses for each company based on customer reviews. Which? Magazine makes annual awards for good customer service and publishes the winners on its website (www.which.co.uk).

A useful way to gauge whether a company is worthy of your custom is to search the web for feedback. You'll find horror stories about every firm, but if the complaints are voluminous and consistent enough you should consider whether that bargain package is worth it. Let's face it though; those bargain packages are likely to blind most of us to a provider's poor social skills so, given the proliferation of service providers, price comparison websites are a good place to start. Ofcom has begun an accreditation scheme to sort out the most reliable of these. At time of writing only three have been signed up – www.simplifydigital.co.uk, www.billmonitor.com and www.broadbandchoices.co.uk – and these are audited annually to check that they are accurate and accessible.

Beware the hidden surprises of small print

As soon as a deal tempts you, you should knuckle down to the small print, for it's here that hidden charges lurk. Some companies, for instance, like to punish you financially for not paying your bills by direct debit; others levy a fee for providing an itemised bill rather than a summary. Penalties for late or failed payments will vary from provider to provider, as will early cancellation fees and the amount of notice you must give to end a contract. You might even find yourself charged for cancelling a contract when you have endured the full term.

Ofcom is keen for all such fees to be proclaimed more prominently and reckons that they should reflect the actual costs incurred by the companies. Surprisingly, few firms have rushed to highlight their grasping side in the same jolly font they favour for their headline deals, nor have their levies been noticeably slashed. They could be forced to do both under the Unfair Terms in Consumer Contracts Regulations if Ofcom decided to take action against them. The regulator promises that it will keep an eye on the issue, and the more people who complain about unfair charges, the more notice the authorities will take.

Once you have chosen your cheap deal, checked for hidden stings and authorised the contract you have 10 working days to change your mind. Letters of regret from your old provider and of rejoicings from their usurper should inform you of this, and the latter should spell out any terms and conditions that might change your view of the package. You should get these in writing, even if the contract was agreed verbally over the telephone. Sick as you are of small print, squint through the company's code of practice because these can vary widely from provider to provider and will give you an idea of their moral fibre. Codes dictate, for instance, how much grace you will be granted before being disconnected for non-payment, how easy it is to make a complaint, what compensation you will be paid if you are cut off, and how long you can expect to wait for a repair.

Slamming – a uniquely modern suspense story

Just possibly you will find yourselves in the arms of a stranger without having signed up to anything. This is called 'slamming', an uncomfortable ordeal akin to Erroneous Transfers in the utilities industry. You have to sympathise with the offenders – it's a hard-hearted market out there, and if the public doesn't heed their allure it's an understandable temptation to force their custom by kidnapping them from their chosen provider. You might not discover your fate until mysterious bills start arriving, including penalties from your old provider for defecting mid-contract. If you are a victim, or if you find that you have been signed up to a service under false pretences – cash back that never materialised, a free trial deal that turned out to be pricey captivity – Ofcom would like to hear from you (there's a form you can fill out at www.ofcom.org.uk).

Mobile phones

The adventures described above are more likely to befall mobile phone customers who must navigate their way through a perplexity of service providers, network providers and third-party dealers. Mis-selling is so rife – it makes up a fifth of all complaints to Ofcom – that the regulator has imposed new rules that came into force in September 2009. All mobile phone companies must now record sales calls, warn potential customers that their old provider may levy a termination charge if they agree to switch, simplify the deliberately complicated process for claiming cash-back offers and hand over all necessary information about a contract at the point of sale. Moreover, service providers must keep a parental eye on dealers authorised to sell their products to make sure that they are behaving.

These reassurances will come too late for the many who have been sweet-talked into an unsuitable deal during an unexpected phone call. Many reputable dealers are authorised by service providers such as Orange to upgrade clients, and they are allowed access to certain customer account details. They can offer an improved package only when an old contract is coming to an end and, once signed up, your contract is with the service provider, not the dealer.

Some dealers, however, do not let the fact that they are unauthorised get in the way. They may claim to represent a familiar high street name to reassure you, and, after you have unwittingly let slip details of your current package (they are adept at canny questioning), they will conjure a rival deal to seduce you. An ex-call-centre operative who had been employed by one notorious firm once explained to me how it works on the inside. She worked 12-hour shifts, calling names on a database that was so out of date that she regularly rang for people who had died. 'The sales target was very high – the two floors of the call centre were pitted against each other – and to reach it people would mislead customers, the favourite ruse being to tell them they'd won a mobile.' Sales staff would claim that they were calling from BT and would quote falsely low charges to entice their prey.

So, when your evening meal is gate-crashed by an excitable youth informing you that you are entitled to gold-star pampering, be cautious. If he claims to act on behalf of your service provider, ask for something in writing before committing yourself and check your existing contract to see if you are due an upgrade (remember if you accept one you will be locked into a new 12- to 18-month contract). If he asks for your address (clever ones will ask you to confirm it, implying that it's already there in front of them), be suspicious. The Distance Selling Regulations will protect you from your folly if you succumb then repent. As long as you agreed the contract over the phone or by mail order and as long as you did not ask for the service to start immediately, you have seven working days to change your mind and request a refund.

Similarly, if you order a handset from home you can cancel without penalty within seven working days of the transaction or within seven working days of receipt.

If you insist on a phone that works...

There is always the chance that the said handset is handsome, savvy and all you've ever dreamed of... it's just that it doesn't work. Perhaps it works, but a few small clues suggest that it is not the pure new gadget you thought you were paying for. A reader found his full of someone else's phone numbers while Pamela Anderson languished across the display screen. When he tried to change her for a more restful image he discovered a portfolio of hardcore porn and a screensaver featuring Garfield rogering a dog.

In either situation you are protected by the Sale of Goods Act and should ask for a repair or a replacement from the retailer. If they refuse, write to them declaring that the phone is not of 'satisfactory quality' and that if they do not repair or replace according to the Sale of Goods Act you will take your case to the small claims court. Ideally, you will have paid by credit card, so, if the rogue plays dead, you can claim off your card issuer under Section 74 of the Consumer Credit Act.

Unfortunately, third-party dealers are not regulated by Ofcom and cannot be disciplined by the telecoms arbitration schemes, so, if you have received shoddy service from one, you can ask the service provider they signed you up to for help. If they can't – or won't – you can notify the regulator or trading standards. Ofcom can't rein in your foe, but under its new rules it can check whether the service provider has vetted its authorised dealers thoroughly enough.

Contract crawling: how to get the best deal

Mobile handsets are appealing-looking fellows these days, but the sleekest, priciest of them are only as good as the network service provider that operates them. Before surrendering yourself to an omnipotent black wafer, therefore, pick the brains of neighbours, friends and forums to find out which provider gives the best service in your local area. If you choose a monthly tariff over pay-as-you-go you will enter a fixed contract from which you can escape only by paying a large penalty, although this mustn't exceed the total charges for the remaining months. This contract could be with one of the following: the network operator that enables calls (there are currently five of these – Orange, T-Mobile, O2, 3 and Vodafone); the service provider that buys airtime from the network operators and sells it on, often under its own brand, such as BT Mobile, Virgin and Tesco; or the retailer that sold you the phone (which might also be the service provider or an agent acting for them).

'No' doesn't always mean 'no': how to escape a soured relationship

So far so snug, until the too-good-to-be-true tariff you unearthed suddenly soars and you find discarded providers look more alluring. If the increase causes you 'material detriment' you should be able to cancel your contract without penalty within a month of being notified, even if you are still tied in. If, alas, the rise does not exceed the Retail Price Index, the official measure for cost of living increases, then you are stuck with it until your term ends and you can defect. Before you storm off, it's worth trying to coax a better deal out of your provider. Tell them that you will leave if they don't match the tariffs of their cheapest rival and their benevolence might startle you.

If, on the other hand, you do decide to cancel, many hours of entertainment may be coming your way. Obviously companies dislike the idea of losing customers, but often they are too idle or too stingy to offer incentives to retain them. Deafness is the answer. There will ensue an ongoing symmetry between your pleas for release and the bills that arrive monthly for a service you can't shake off. This is where your entanglement with both a mobile network operator and a mobile service provider can become impenetrable.

One reader bought a phone through Phones 4u but decided to cancel the contract within the cooling-off period. He received, however, merciless invoices from Orange for a service he had never used. Phones 4u admitted that it had failed to cancel his contract properly; Orange acknowledged that it had no business hanging on to his money, and both sides agreed that he should be refunded and released. But the bills kept on coming. He rang Orange, which blamed Phones 4u; he rang Phones 4u, which blamed Orange. 'Each party claimed that they were unwilling or unable to contact the other or that the other party was unwilling to discuss the matter,' he said. The 'debt' was eventually sold to a collection agency, and from this point Orange refused to speak to the customer and Phones 4u declared itself unable to speak to third parties. He had, of course fallen prey to a tactic beloved of big corporations when more than one firm is involved: blame each other and hope the piggy in the middle goes away.

When you cancel a contract, do so in writing and send it recorded delivery so that the company can't accuse you of fantasising. You should not have to give more than 30 days' notice under Ofcom rules. If bills continue to rain through your letterbox after the deadline, call the company to protest and follow this up with a letter confirming the conversation. Then call your bank and cancel any direct debits to the phone company. (If you are disputing the amount of a final bill write a cheque for the amount you believe you owe and send it with an explanatory letter.) Just possibly a conciliatory sum will already be on its way to you; equally likely is the need for another telephone call and another letter from you setting out what you want and why.

Corporate deafness: remedies to try at home

Each telecoms company operates its own complaints procedure – a tedious and time-consuming hike through various layers of management – and you have to submit to this before anyone else will take you seriously. Details of each process will be in the code of practice on the company's website. Once you can rise no further and your refund has still not arrived you should ask for a 'letter of deadlock' (an admission that they are washing their hands of you) so that you can transfer your grievance for free to an Alternative Dispute Resolution Scheme. All companies must now be a member of one of two approved schemes: the telecommunications ombudsman, Otelo (www.otelo.org.uk), or the Communications and Internet Services Adjudication Scheme, CISAS (www.cisas.org.uk). The company's website should tell you which one they are signed up to, and both schemes' websites list their members. You can seek refuge with one of these schemes without a letter of deadlock, but only after eight fruitless weeks have elapsed since your first complaint. The adjudicators will mediate on your behalf as long as your case falls within their remit, and they have the power to award you a goodwill payment if they feel you have suffered material loss. Make sure you have a functioning photocopier to hand because they will require copious amounts of paperwork and will not return originals. Often the telecoms company will capitulate once the adjudicators start dogging them. If they don't, the process can drag on for several weeks and if, at the end of it, you are unhappy with the official conclusion you can complain to Ofcom or to Otelo's independent adjudicator about how your case was handled.

Internet service providers

By the time you read this you should have worked out whether to surf courtesy of a dial-up or broadband service and will have hazarded your own way through the tangle of ADSL, Cable and Local Loop Unbundled broadband, not to mention satellite, wi-fi and wi-Max options (if you are mystified go to www.ofcom.org. uk/consumeradvice/internet/service/overview/ for a translation). That's the easy bit. In fact, for half of UK households the choice is simplified because they are not reached by the cable network. A minority of others insist on living so far from a BT exchange that they can't get broadband at all and therefore miss out on some of the extraordinary adventures that entertain the rest of us. These are not necessarily online adventures. The thrills of the internet can seem pretty tame stuff compared to the battles to get on to it in the first place.

Cyber adventures: finding that first relationship

The dullest experiences go something like this. Person decides to get broadband or to switch their internet service provider. They turn to a price comparison website (Ofcom accredits two; see above) to find out which services are available in their area and which offer the cheapest deal. Being canny, the person is not blinded by pushy bargains. Instead, they check out the connection speed and connection charges of their chosen service, any inconvenient download limits, what kind of service they can expect (the price comparison uswitch.com offers a guide to each company's behaviour based on customer feedback) and, crucially, the cheapness and availability of technical support in case there is a difficulty. A budget deal might not seem quite so enriching when you find you have to dangle on a 50p a minute helpline to report a problem.

The person then contacts their existing supplier, if they have one, and asks for a migration authorisation code (MAC), a magic formula that should waft them seamlessly into the arms of their new provider. If they want to transfer their broadband and telephone service together they don't need one of these; they simply have to tell their chosen provider that they want to defect and, magically, two letters, one from the old supplier and one from the new, will arrive confirming the intended transfer. Within ten days the happy person should be up and running with the rival.

Increasingly, since the regulator introduced rules governing broadband switching, this does happen. But this book is concerned with the times that it doesn't. And, unhappily, those times are still rife enough to fuel multiple chapters.

Cyber adventures: the darker side

Most of the problems involving internet service providers boil down to two issues: overstretched, inadequately staffed customer services and an almost touching reluctance to see a good customer depart. Talk Talk, for instance, informed a newly deceased subscriber that since he had signed an 18-month contract, his account could not be transferred into his wife's name. A particular grievance among service providers is customers who insist on defecting to a rival because their internet connection has ceased to work, assuming it functioned in the first place – the fact that a particular service is not available in a particular area is not reason enough for some companies to refuse an order. The fault often occurs because the provider has devoured smaller rivals and, in transferring their customers to its own network, inadvertently sheds numbers of them along the way. Others are victims of systems upgrades that boot them out of cyberspace.

Pointing this out to the offender requires deep pockets and angelic patience. The law does not care what service providers charge for support, provided they make their charges clear and don't abuse premium-rate regulations. One customer reckoned to have spent over £120 over several weeks ringing BT's helpline to report a non-functioning broadband connection, only to discover that the fault was at BT's end – it didn't have enough lines to supply him. Meanwhile, Virgin Media decided to transform its free helpline to a 25p-a-minute earner with a 10p connection charge, which meant that the more unreliable its service became the more people would have to pay to complain. Customers may get their money back if their problem turns out to be Virgin's fault, but only, Virgin told me, if their customer services staff feel munificent.

Cyber adventures: the struggle to flee

Happily for the providers, there exists a sturdy manacle with which they can tether restless customers. This is the aforementioned MAC, without which individuals cannot migrate to another company, unless they are a cable customer, signed up to a Local Loop Unbundled network or are transferring a broadband and telephone package. Ironically, MACs were devised to protect us all by speeding up the transfer process and preventing unscrupulous firms from stealing our custom, but until 2007 providers only had to issue them if they felt like it, and, given that the consequence would be lost customers, many of them never did feel like it.

In 2007 Ofcom changed the rules, so that a provider must reveal the magic formula within five working days of being asked for it, whether or not the customer has debts or is tied into a contract, and the code should remain valid for 30 days. In reality, however, companies devise ingenious excuses for withholding it. Homecall, now part of Tiscali, was aghast when a couple who had spent three months trying to get a functioning service wrote asking for their contract to be terminated. Professing incredulity, it asked them to send an email confirming their treachery. Without a functioning broadband service this was difficult and when, a few days later, the couple did so, they found that Homecall had, in the meantime, belatedly bestirred itself and activated their broadband, which meant that they could no longer cancel without penalty.

Deafness and amnesia are other favourite tactics to deny customers their escape code. Your only weaponry in this case is pen and ink in repeated quantities, then, once you've exhausted the in-house complaints procedure and still not got anywhere, you should notify Ofcom to allow them to enforce its own rules.

If and when a MAC trundles your way grab it quickly before it expires and be sure to tell your new provider that you want a seamless switch, otherwise you face a week or more without service when your old provider releases you. Moreover, no matter how detestable you find the old foe, don't place a cease order while the transfer is taking place. Otherwise, they will place a tag on your line, and this will prevent the new service from starting up until after the old one has run its course. Only once you are safely up and running with your new provider should you confirm in writing that you want the old account terminated. It is worth remembering to do this because telecoms companies have notoriously shaky memories and are perfectly capable of billing you in tandem with your new choice until you get round to studying your bank statements.

Local Loop Unbundling and other adventures

Sadly, Ofcom's new rules have not yet liberated those who have signed up to a Local Loop Unbundled (LLU) package – that is, to a provider that has installed its own equipment in a BT exchange and supplies broadband directly to its customers. This technical wizardry is supposed to speed up connection speeds and, because the companies no longer have to lease lines from BT, it produces cheap – or even free – broadband deals. In reality, however, it often dumps customers altogether because the transfer process from ASDL lines to LLU is still evolving. Escaping from an LLU provider can be a suspenseful ordeal because if you return to an ASDL service you have to be manually transferred back to the BT network, which means that you may lose your broadband service for a period and will probably have to pay a fee. (If you'd moved your telephone to LLU too you'll have to pay a reconnection fee of £124.99 to BT.) Even switching from one LLU provider to another can be tormenting because you'll be restricted to a narrow range of companies that supply broadband from your local exchange. Not all LLU providers offer MACs, and not all service providers accept the MACs of those that do because LLU MACs are different from the ordinary kind. If your chosen provider doesn't accept your code you will have to cancel, disconnect your LLU line and pay a fee to the new firm for setting up a new connection. Because the process is so tricky, it's worth checking out what is expected of you from both your old and your new providers before embarking on the adventure – some unfortunates have found themselves billed simultaneously by two companies because they got the transfer procedures wrong.

Fixed contracts: how to break free unscathed

It's quite possible that your provider, be it ASDL, cable or LLU, declines to lose you because you are halfway through a fixed contract. This is reasonable enough if you are receiving the service you are paying for. But say that, for instance, your broadband has been lifeless for three months while the bills churn out with cruelly contrasting vigour. And say that, despite long hours on the 25p-a-minute helpline and long letters to the customer services department, the company has failed to lift a finger to help you. In that case you can legally disengage yourself without liability. Most contracts contain, buried deep within them, a termination clause that allows you to flee without penalty if you receive no service for a sustained period, which is usually around four weeks. You need to warn your provider in writing that you intend to invoke this clause if four weeks passes without a resolution, otherwise things could turn against you should your case reach the courts.

If your contract omits this useful opt-out you can still get out of it if you are not receiving the service you are paying for. If, for instance, your provider decides to up- or downgrade your package without warning, then scuttles into hiding, farewells are justified no matter how long your tie-in period. It's all a matter of terminology. Don't write that you are cancelling your contract. Instead, say that you are repudiating it because the firm is in breach of its conditions and demand that they send a refund within 28 days for the period that you've been without service. If this is not forthcoming – and there's no reason to suppose it will be, given your previous sufferings – you can mention the small claims court, or, provided you have waited 12 weeks or received a letter of deadlock, you can take your lament to the dispute resolution schemes CISAS or OTELO.

Once you have repudiated a contract you can cancel your direct debit payments (the company won't like this, and you should brace yourself for menacing letters) and begin a search for a friendlier firm. A word of warning here: avoid at all costs authorising monthly deductions from your credit card to pay for any kind of service.

This is known as a continuing payment authority, and it is dangerously different from a direct debit because neither you nor your bank can cancel the payments without the agreement of the retailer. Not even cancelling your credit card will help if the retailer declines to lose your custom. You can raise a dispute with your card issuer, but it could take up to six months to resolve, and you will be shelling out impotently in the meantime.

Tips for scarred escapees: how to hang on to your liberty

Once you have recovered from the above battles you may feel nervous about intimacy with a new provider, but there is a way around this. You do not always have to commit the next two years of your life to a company when you sign up to their broadband service; there are deals with no contracted minimum term or with only three-month tie-ins. So far so marvellous, but beware the small print. Providers have to pay a fee to BT to lease their lines, but will often connect contracted customers for free because they know they'll have the next year or two to wring money out of them. If there is no contract the provider may charge this sum up-front or, if you decide to seek juicier pastures two months on, your provider will demand the money before you leave to recoup the costs of connecting an ingrate.

Even more intoxicating are the deals that boast of having no connection fee. Heady stuff indeed if you remain loyal, but should you decide to look elsewhere within 12 months, even though you are not contracted to a minimum term, you should be braced for a cancellation charge, although this may well be less than the penalty you would pay for breaking a fixed contract early.

Whenever you feel the need to tangle with telecoms firms the safest precaution is cynicism. They will tempt you with free laptops, huge cash-back sums, dizzying connection speeds and possibly a cruise for two to Jutland. Flattering as these attentions are, you must rein in your excitement and remember that these are not gifts; they are bait. By the time you have survived a two-year contract with higher than average premiums you will have funded half a dozen laptops and missed out on cheaper, better deals elsewhere. The dense pages of terms and conditions are far more revelatory about a deal than the excitable headlines. Read the small print, do your sums and remember the old cliché: if a thing looks too good to be true, it probably is.

CHECKLIST

- You can find the best deals for mobile, landline and broadband on price comparison websites, but before you sign up check for hidden charges buried in the small print that could distort the bargain.
- Reliability is worth more than a cheap deal. Comparison websites, such as uswitch and www.topcomm.org.uk, give feedback about the quality of each company's customer services.

- When you agree to a deal over the telephone you should receive the contract in writing and you have a seven-day cooling-off period.
- Be wary of unsolicited calls from third-party dealers. Ask for offers to be confirmed in writing before you commit yourself.
- You can get out of a contract without penalty if the terms and conditions are significantly breached or if they change to your material detriment. Advise the company in writing that you intend to invoke the termination clause because they are in breach of contract.
- Internet service providers are obliged to send you a migration authorisation code (MAC) within five working days of your request to enable you to switch companies.
- If you switch providers always confirm the cancellation of a contract by letter and send it recorded delivery.
- Keep a chronological file of bank statements and bills and other related paperwork in case there is a dispute about charges.
- When things go wrong find out about the company's in-house complaints procedure. Once you have followed this, you can take your case to an alternative dispute resolution scheme within eight weeks of the first complaint or sooner if you receive a letter of deadlock from the company.

9
Postal services

Matt Thompson of North Berwick was careful to take out extra insurance when he entrusted a £500 microphone to Parcel Force. The package was never seen again. Thompson was assured that a search had been started and that he should wait to hear from customer services. Parcel Force's terms and conditions state that claims for compensation must be made within 30 days, so when the deadline approached Thompson asked what he should do. He was told not to worry because the search was still under way. The rest is predictable. After many further calls and fob-offs, he put in a claim and was told that because he was outside the 30-day period there was no record of his calls and faxes and that his claim was no longer valid. Later he read in Parcel Force's terms and conditions that all records of its activities are destroyed after a month. 'All I was doing was taking them at their word that they were searching for my property,' he said. 'In fact, it was busy shredding any evidence that I'd sent the parcel in the first place.'

If you crave suspense, adventure and intimate relations with strangers you need travel no further than your local pillar box. For best results, take with you something of scant monetary value but significant personal import. The infant cardigan you've spent the last three months knitting, for instance, or your not-quite-yet overdue tax return. Then poke it into that slit of darkness. That's the suspense part. It may reach its destination whole and intact before said infant reaches manhood . . . or it may not. The adventure and the intimacy begin when it does not, and you spend the ensuing weeks having not-so-sweet nothings purred at you by call-centre staff.

Looking back over my hundreds of columns it's surprising that postal sagas are not more dominating. A Which? survey a couple of years ago found that customers disliked Royal Mail and the Post Office even more than banks, broadband providers and mobile phone companies, with only one in five reckoning themselves satisfied with its services. Quite why the prejudice is so strong is an absorbing question. After all, the majority of our post reaches its destination for one of the lowest fees in Europe. Most of that majority even arrives on time, more or less. The minority of stuff that doesn't make it, however, exposes the rot. It's not just the fact that our first-class franked bank statement tours the Northern Isles for a week before it reaches us – when a company handles 83 million items a day it would be miraculous if nothing ever went astray. No, it's the fact that when packages arrive late or mangled or not at all, it can require unusual tenacity to get anything done about it.

The Universal Service Obligation and why it doesn't mean universal service

The Universal Service Obligation (USO) is a statutory millstone that torments Royal Mail, for it requires the organisation to deliver post to every UK address every working day for a flat, capped fee. It is also legally bound to collect post from even the remotest pillar boxes six days a week. An expensive bore, this, that interferes distressingly with the business of making a profit. Rival companies, which since 2006 have been let loose to collect, sort and deliver bulk mail, are unfettered by this obligation, and although a government-appointed regulator, Postcomm, was set up to ensure that Royal Mail abides by the USO, it seems that the company has canny strategies to get round it.

An Edinburgh postman once contacted me to point out that the USO is routinely ignored. 'Royal Mail gets round the obligation by counting as delivered all mail that leaves the delivery office,' he said. 'A part-timer is given mail they can't hope to deliver by the end of their shift so they dump it in a post box, but it's counted as delivered.' The postman reckoned Royal Mail uses misleading delivery statistics to justify job cuts, compounding the problem whereby 'managers are paid for achieving targets reached only on paper'. 'In one delivery office where I work, 43 walks were reduced to 28 and full-time workers were replaced with part-timers,' he told me.

Postal workers can legitimately return undelivered

post to collection boxes if they run out of time, but Royal Mail insists that this is rare and that if a worker cannot shift their load on a three-and-a-half hour round, someone will be appointed to finish it for them (odd, then, that my area had no mail for a week because there was no cover for a sick postwoman). However, the postal watchdog Postwatch, now Consumer Focus, told me that USO failures could be far more widespread than official figures show because, since it is so difficult to get through to Royal Mail's customer services, many complaints go unreported.

Why the customer is always wrong

The costly struggle required to gain the ear of postal officials is a common theme running through the complaints that come my way. When, in response to a 'Sorry you were out' delivery notice, did you last try ringing the delivery office number on the back? If, when you finally defeated the engaged tones, someone actually answered, you experienced a minor miracle. It's more likely that you trekked to some grim outer reaches of your home town, queued for 20 minutes and waited a further 10 while an official ran a forefinger down the pages of an immense, hand-scrawled ledger to find your entry (computer technology has not yet made it to provincial depots; not where I live anyway). With a bit of luck your package was retrieved. Or possibly not.

One reader discovered that her undelivered package had been lost after it had been returned to the depot, and, since it had been dispatched from the United States, Royal Mail insisted that it was the responsibility of the US postal services to compensate her for its own carelessness. The US naturally figured that since the parcel had reached its destination, albeit fleetingly, it had nothing to do with the problem.

Royal Mail, as we all know, is struggling with its finances. Given its terrifying pension deficit and the rival challenge of electronic mail, it is unsurprising that it does not wish to waste spare pennies on pacifying whingers. It and its subsidiary sister company Parcel Force have therefore perfected a tool to excuse them from liability: if something goes wrong, blame the customer. One man wrote to me after a rare dynamo from a vintage car had reached its destination smashed almost to pieces. Not only had he followed Parcel Force's own guidelines and swaddled it in bubblewrap, newspaper and cardboard, but the recipient had kept the packaging and shown them to an official inspector. The sender had insured the device for up to £250, but Parcel Force refused to pay up because, it said, it had been inadequately wrapped. He asked to see the inspector's report and was told that it could neither be sent nor read out to him over the phone. He was given a contact name to complain to, but she failed to reply to his letter and, he was told, 'she does not speak on the phone'.

Dodgy packaging is a favourite excuse that saves the Royal Mail Group millions of pounds of insurance payments every year. Many people do skimp on wrappings, but Consumer Focus reckons that Post Office counter staff should assess each parcel when it is handed over and, once they have accepted it, Royal Mail or Parcel Force should be responsible for its wellbeing.

Innocents might assume that recorded delivery would protect them from some of the mischief that befalls items in transit. It offers, at least, confirmation that the goods have reached their destination. But, as a Royal Mail spokesman explained to me with unconscious irony: 'It is operationally impossible for Royal Mail to keep records of items sent recorded delivery.' Which is why a reader who prudently sent his tax return and other vital paperwork recorded delivery found that of the five envelopes dispatched, only one generated a signature. He complained and received a reply stating that unless he responded within five days the case would be closed. The letter added that since the addressee of two of the missing items had not answered Royal Mail's inquiry about whether the letters had been received, he should chase them up himself. Happily, he came by a booklet called *Keeping Our Promise*, in which Royal Mail invites customers who are dissatisfied with the outcome of a complaint to ring a given number and ask to speak to a manager. He did so and was informed that he was not allowed to speak directly to one of these elevated beings.

The idea, of course, is to design a customer-repelling process that thwarts all but the most determined attempts to complain. When utilities or telecoms companies behave like this we can at least choose to flee to a more empathetic rival. With postal services, however, unless we are a small business sending out several thousand items of post a year, we are stuck with Royal Mail, which still handles over 97 per cent of deliveries. That being so, we must learn to make the best of it, and the more diligently we do so, the better we can protect ourselves.

How to survive the British postal system

Lesson one is to fathom postal linguistics. Take recorded delivery, for instance. You might assume that the delivery will be recorded so that you know your treasure has arrived safely and that, indeed, if it makes it to the correct doorstep you are likely to receive a confirmatory squiggle. If it doesn't, however, you are no better off than you would have been if you'd saved the money and sent it by ordinary post. The oft misunderstood fact is that recorded delivery items travel along with first- and second-class mail, and their journeys are not tracked. The customer is simply paying extra for a signature at the door, and if this is not achieved they should get the money back. A word of warning here. Always check that the packaging is in good shape before signing for a delivery because Royal Mail and other delivery firms often refuse to compensate for damaged goods if they are signed for.

If your envelope contains a sheaf of gift vouchers for your grandchildren, a small family heirloom or anything of monetary value then you should never use recorded delivery because Royal Mail cannot guarantee its safety and is exempted from compensating you if it goes missing. Instead, you should pay a surplus for special delivery, which ensures that the item is tracked along its way and, unless it is destined for a far-flung Scottish island, arrives by 1 p.m. the following day (you get your money back if it doesn't). You are entitled to up to £500 (£50 if you choose the next day 9 a.m. service) if it is lost or damaged and can pay extra to insure it for a maximum of £2,500. If your package contains a vital contract or a tax return that will cost you dear if it goes astray, you can add still more to the postage to cover yourself for consequential loss.

Post destined for abroad remains the responsibility of Royal Mail even when it's left these shores, and if it vanishes on foreign soil it is Royal Mail that must compensate you (similarly items posted to the UK from abroad are the responsibility of that country's postal service until they reach their destination). At time of writing you can receive up to £34 for lost valuables but, unless you are sending a mobile phone or money in some form, you can buy extra insurance to cover them up to £250 or £500, depending on the country they are bound for. It's worth forking out the small fee for the international advice of delivery service, which provides written proof of delivery.

It's sensible to explain to Post Office counter staff what is in a package before you send it so they can advise you about the most suitable service and, while they are at it, check whether the packaging is robust enough to survive Royal Mail's sometimes less than tender handling. There are descriptions of the often fearful quantities of swaddling required for different kinds of goods on the company's website (www.royalmail.com).

Before you surrender it to its destiny make sure you write a return address on the envelope or wrappings so that it might make its way back to you if the adventure goes wrong. And then, if it is travelling by ordinary mail, ask for a receipt proving when and where you posted it. This will help you in your battle for compensation if the item is never seen again, and battle you must because the more money Royal Mail has to pay out the more care it will take of its charges. When your laboriously written but valueless thank-you notelet shreds or vanishes in transit you are entitled to minimum redress of six first-class stamps under the Retail Compensation Scheme introduced by Postcomm in August 2008. If it's delayed by more than three days you should expect the same consolation. You can request compensation forms from any post office or from Royal Mail's website.

If, say, a box set of DVDs was tucked in with the notelet and you can produce proof of its value and of postage you would get your postage refunded, plus compensation up to the maximum market value of the discs or 100 first-class stamps, whichever is cheaper. If you don't have proof of posting you're back to those six stamps.

All these useful and enjoyable precautions count for naught, however, when you are the recipient and have no choice over how the sender decides to dispatch the parcel. This matters if, for instance, the goods are Christmas presents ordered by you from an online retailer. Unless you requested special or even recorded delivery, proving that you have not received something is a good deal more challenging than proving that you sent it. Moreover, the delivery firm's contract is with the sender, so you cannot elicit compensation directly from the former. If the retailer is a reputable one it will resend or refund the item, then fight its own battles with the culprit. When a website gives you the option of paying extra for special delivery, suppress that perfectly natural stinginess and fork out so that you are better protected if your consumer durables go missing.

The hidden stings of foreign bounty

There may come a time when you are surprised by a postman bearing a thrilling-looking package ornamented with exotic stamps. All yours, he tells you amiably, provided you hand over £8. If you do not do so the parcel will be borne off untouched. In most other situations this would be called a ransom. Delivery companies term it a customs clearance fee and levy it on goods worth over £18 (£36 if it's a personal gift from one individual to another) sent from abroad when HM Revenue & Customs imposes duty or VAT on it.

Customs fees have distressed readers more than almost any other element of postal services. So many aspects of the process are unfair. You might, for instance, not have solicited or expected the parcel with which your grandmother in Brisbane decided to surprise you, in which case you have no opportunity to decide whether you want to surrender £8 (unless you refuse the present on the doorstep). Even if the package contains something you ordered from an overseas retailer you have no choice over which delivery company the retailer selects, and clearance fees can vary between firms from £8 to as much as £25. Moreover, many websites fail to point out that you will be liable for a levy that will sour your bargain.

Delivery companies argue that the fee reflects the costs involved in nursing a parcel through customs, including paying duty and taxes, shifting paperwork and, brazenly, processing the clearance fee when it's been extorted from the recipient. All you, the recipient, can do is study HM Revenue & Customs charges before succumbing to that bargain from the US and warn granny not to be too lavish with her gifts in future.

Junking junk mail

There are times when it is to our advantage if mail addressed to us never reaches our letterbox. Quite probably there are souls whose lives are so deprived of colour and purpose that they welcome the rainbow-hued envelopes that clog their doormats and invite them to collect vast winnings (for a fee) from a Canadian lottery they have never heard of or have their health, wealth and sex life consolidated (for a fee) by a soothsayer in Worthing. For most of us, however, junk mail is an personal irritant and an environmental scandal, but for delivery companies it represents profits as dazzling as its promises.

One Dorset couple who signed up for Royal Mail's redirection service while they spent three weeks in Wales found that their post was delivered faithfully to Dorset during their Celtic holiday, then shifted to Wales once they had returned home. This was not particularly surprising, as many of you who have sampled the redirection service will testify. No, the unexpected part was that Royal Mail had evidently sold the couple's name and temporary address to other companies, so that their elderly Welsh friends found themselves bombarded with junk mail addressed to their guests. All parties tried repeatedly to stem the flow, but Royal Mail seemed unable or unwilling to act. The couple were victims of a tiny box concealed in the small print of the redirection forms. This has to be ticked by customers who do not want their details sold to all and sundry – that is, customers have to opt out of bombardment rather than opt in, which, morally, is the wrong way around but works out very lucratively for Royal Mail.

In the likely event that you resent lurid clutter filling your recycling box, you can sign up to the Mailing Preference Service (www.mpsonline.org.uk or 0845 703 4599), which will shield you from all but overseas nuisances. Ignore overtures from companies offering to perform this favour for a fee; the Mailing Preference Service is thorough and free. It won't stop unaddressed correspondence directed to The Occupier, which is delivered in bulk by Royal Mail. There is, however, an opt-out that Royal Mail keeps so quiet that many of its own staff are unaware of it. The secret information is an address: Freepost RRBT-ZBXB-TTTS, Royal Mail Door to Door Opt Outs, Kingsmead House, Oxpens Road, Oxford OX1 1RX or email optout@royalmail.com. You will be sent a form to fill in and return, and the circulars should peter out within six weeks, although be aware you may miss out on important notifications.

The power of protest and how when and where to unleash it

Inertia will prevent most of us from filing an official complaint, and inertia makes sure that when a first-class letter arrives three days late we fascinate dinner party guests with our grievance, but fail to complain to Royal Mail. It's important, though, that we add any laments to all the others that pour in because both watchdog and regulator rely on customer feedback to help gauge whether Royal Mail is fulfilling its brief.

You don't need to spend the afternoon in the customer services queue; complaints can be posted to Royal Mail Customer Service Centre, FREEPOST, 20 Turner Road, St Rollox Retail and Business Park, Glasgow G21 1AA or emailed to contactus@ royalmail.com. The company says it aims to reply within 30 days, and you have a fortnight to respond to its response. If all goes quiet or if the reply skirts the issue, you start moving up a four-runged ladder. The second rung is referral to the customer services manager, then, if their ministrations don't pacify you, to the customer services director's office, then finally to the Royal Mail's Postal Review panel (postalreview@royalmail.com). At this point, or 90 days after your first contact, if the problem still cannot be resolved, the company will wash its hands of you – the elegant term is a letter of deadlock, which is your passport to the next stage – the Independent Postal Redress Scheme (www.POSTRS.org.uk). You can fast forward to this point if Royal Mail or other member delivery companies fail to follow their own complaints procedures correctly. The scheme, currently the only one approved by the regulator Postcomm, offers free independent arbitration between you and nine licensed delivery companies and can award up to £50 for stress and inconvenience plus standard compensation for any loss or damage.

Unfortunately, the scheme can rule only on activities licensed by Postcomm, which does not regulate either Post Office Ltd or Parcel Force, so if you are complaining about either of these your last option is legal action through the small claims court. Once you've forwarded your paperwork it will respond to you within six weeks of your first contact, and you must accept or reject their conclusions within four weeks, otherwise the offending company will not be bound by them.

Your foe must then act on the arbitrators' decision before another four weeks is up, otherwise the arbitrators will embark on a series of solemn internal meetings and work out what, if anything, they can do about it.

This safety net is wonderfully reassuring for those thwarted by delivery companies' own less than empathetic customer services procedures. There's only one remaining problem: you have to rely on Royal Mail to deliver all the vital paperwork to and from the arbitrators!

CHECKLIST

- Always tell Post Office counter staff what's in a parcel so they can assess the packaging and suggest the most suitable service.
- Valuable items cannot be sent recorded delivery. If they are worth more than £34 you must pay extra for special delivery, which tracks the item, guarantees next-day arrival and pays up to £500 compensation if it is lost or damaged.
- For an extra fee you can insure parcels for up to £2,500 and buy cover for consequential loss.
- Make sure you ask for proof of posting, otherwise you may not receive full compensation if your item is lost, delayed or damaged.
- Always check the packaging of goods as soon as they are handed over because some delivery companies won't compensate for damage if you have signed for the package.

- Post sent abroad remains the responsibility of Royal Mail even after it's left the UK; the relevant overseas delivery company is liable for post sent to the UK from abroad. If valuables are lost overseas you can claim up to £34 or else pay to insure them for up to £500, depending on the item and its destination.

- For UK post six first-class stamps are the minimum compensation if letters posted first or second class or recorded delivery get lost or damaged. If the item has intrinsic value you can claim up to 100 first-class stamps or the market value, whichever is lower, provided you have proof of postage and its value.

- If you are ordering goods from abroad you may incur customs clearance fees, which range from £8 to £25.

- Junk mail can be stopped by signing up to the Mailing Preference Service at www.mpsonline.org.uk

- Complaints should always follow the delivery company's own complaints procedures as detailed on their website. If you reach a deadlock you can refer your grievance to the Independent Postal Redress Scheme (www.POSTRS.org.uk), but this does not cover unlicensed operations, such as Parcel Force and Post Office Ltd.

Awards

The companies that have worked so hard to keep my postbag full for 12 years deserve an acknowledgment for their trouble. Here then, with due pomp, is a list of awards to mark the most remarkable interpretations of customer service over the years.

Worst customer services

There are so many contenders for this one. British Gas and British Telecom have given it their best shots, and Ikea and Moben have support networks that are hard to beat. But Ryanair, whose response to one of my inquiries was that international regulations didn't apply to it, and which forces passengers to pay 10p a minute to queue on its customer service line (it doesn't publish email addresses) and then ignores their laments, has to be the favourite. It refused to fly home a 'homeless' backpacker whose tent and rucksack it had lost; it declined liability for damage to luggage with wheels or handles – in other words, most suitcases; when demand proved limited for its Pisa flights it renamed the airport

Florence; and it told a disabled passenger that a wheelchair was a 'frill'.

Most surreal excuse
Why was a tombstone commissioned by a reader delayed by six months without word? Because, explained the Memorial Firm, of a 'skeleton staff' following the death of a quarry worker. 'We didn't notify the customer of the delay,' said a spokesman, 'because, since we are in the bereavement business, we didn't like to mention death.'

Best example of corporate logic
Ikea has tried for this prize with innumerable strategies, but my favourite is the case of reader Dermod Quirke, who wanted to buy three of its footstools. 'I was told two were available and 19 were "in air",' he said. This translated as being stranded on a top shelf and retrievable only by forklift truck in the dead of night. Could the required third be fork-lifted overnight and reserved? No, Ikea does not take overnight orders. Could extra numbers be transferred to the lower shelves to meet demand? No, the computer only allows two to descend at a time. To buy three, Quirke would have to make two separate cross-country trips to the store.

Most spectacular climb-down
'If you want a simple wedding with no fuss, it's no problem,' boasted Virgin Holidays' wedding brochure. And, indeed, Virgin made sure that two *Guardian-*

reading couples had a far simpler wedding than they had planned by changing their flight schedules so they would have to shave two days off their festivities. The company declared itself powerless to help the foursome, who had booked a £60,000 double-wedding package in Antigua, until the *Guardian* breathed romance in its ear and, suddenly, it mustered funds to charter a special flight and fly the party from the island on their original departure date.

Canniest profit-booster

There are three winners in this category. TV Licensing invented four different addresses within one apartment block for a valid licence-holder so that it could persecute her for unpaid dues; Three sent an unsolicited handset to a reader, then insisted that, since it had no record of him, he would have to open an account in order to return it; and finally, Thames Water told a customer who was being billed for a stranger's water consumption that the only way to stop the demands was to set up a monthly payment plan.

The ectoplasm award

This goes to a select group of companies that sold goods and services that did not actually exist. Virgin Trains sold a reader a £1,200 season ticket that was valid only on a service that no longer ran. Another reader bought a ticket for a train that existed solely in the imaginations of Virgin's sales team. The online agent, Opodo, tried to sell a reader five tickets for imaginary flights, and a rogue ticket agency, Getmetickets, offered dress-circle seats for the Glastonbury festival.

Biggest cock-up

Tempting as it is to commemorate the couple who spent three years without properly functioning central heating after a British Gas engineer came to fix a radiator valve, or the £6,000 worth of repairs required after the same amiable company installed a new combi boiler, the honour rightfully belongs to Seeboard. Following routine maintenance on the local electricity supply, engineers reconnected Catherine Reay's house with two live wires and no neutral. She cottoned on when she flicked a light switch and her appliances began bursting into flames. 'Seeboard told me that I ought to be grateful that my house was earthed the way it was, otherwise my taps and light switches could have gone live,' she said.

Most convenient excuse

How about the utilities company TXU, which told an overcharged customer: 'Our computers don't automatically send refunds', by which it meant that they weren't configured to send refunds off their own bat. Or npower, which explained that a customer owed £900 had not been paid 'because she was owed so much'. Similarly, Stagecoach Oxford declined to offer compensation to a passenger injured by driver negligence. 'Due to the gravity of the complaint,' it declared, 'compensation would not be appropriate.' Then there is Phones 4u, which refused to reveal the results of an investigation into a customer's complaint. 'These will unfortunately remain within the parameters of Phones 4u,' wrote the customer services manager, 'which I trust demonstrates the gravity we attach to issues of customer services.'

Tardiest service

How many engineers does it take to change a cooker lightbulb? Five over 10 months – and they still didn't manage. Or how about the flight to Cyprus booked through Metak Holidays that took three days? And the Moben kitchen that was meant to take three days to install and was still not complete a year later? Ah, Moben, it deserves a wee prize all of its own: 'The inspector who came to assess the damage wrought by the men who fitted my new kitchen asked if I really needed a sink since I had a dishwasher,' said reader Caroline Reading, who had been left with a sink that could not empty and a dishwasher that drained straight into it.

Most inventive use of the English language award

Definition of call-out charge? Fee charged by labourer for making it to the doorstep. Wrong. As one reader found, if you ask a plumber to examine two appliances on a visit, you are liable for two call-out charges.

Definition of delivery charge? The cost of getting goods from supplier to purchaser. Misleading.

Charmian Bollinger, who ordered two computers from Dell, was assured that there would be no delivery fee. However, £49 was then charged for freight. The difference, Dell explained, is that delivery is the transportation from warehouse to customer, but freight covers the journey from factory to warehouse. 'As far as I'm concerned, free delivery means I pay for the items delivered and nothing more,' protested Bollinger, reasonably enough.

Definition of cancellation? Withdrawal of pre-arranged service. Not according to online booking agency divento.com. Two readers pre-booked timed tickets for an exhibition at the Musée d'Orsay in Paris, but the museum was closed on the relevant day. Divento refused to refund them, claiming that non-opening was not the same as a cancellation.

Best customer-elimination strategy

This is the means by which companies silence bothersome customers who keep demanding their dues. Homecall hit on a winner when it arbitrarily changed a customer's name on its records, then refused to deal with the customer because he was not the named account holder (although it still pocketed his subscription, obviously). Applause, too, for Next, which ordered customer service staff to delete all requests for a call-back to eliminate a three-month backlog. But perhaps the highest accolade should go to ebuyer, which told an empty-handed purchaser that so many (inactive) weeks had elapsed since her complaint had been lodged that the company considered the matter closed and had deleted her file. 'Emails don't work, they don't answer the phone – the only time I managed to get through, I was put on hold for 10 minutes then cut off, and they have a system of eNotes that they don't respond to,' lamented the customer, Yvette Dickinson.

Equal opportunities award
Tricky one this: should it be Direct Line, which quoted Julian Tournier a £7 premium for life insurance, then raised it to £34 when it found out he was gay. 'I don't drink or smoke and have had the same partner for five years, yet Direct Line seems to think I'm some kind of pervert who changes partner every week and who will die of Aids in the next five years,' he told us. Or Airtours, which gave Dr Joanna Smith a sex change on her travel documents because its computers would only recognise a doctor as male. If she wanted to return to her usual gender, she would have to travel as Mrs.

Home improver of the decade award
It would be churlish not to reward Dolphin Bathrooms, which, over the years, has employed vanishing fitters, fitters who don't speak English, fitters who turn up without materials and materials that turn up without fitters. This is what happened when Sara Howers paid the company nearly £10,000 for a makeover. The fitter could not decipher his worksheet; he left a drainpipe disconnected and flooded the kitchen; the electricity supply was off for days because of water leaking into

the power sockets; a door was hung the wrong way round; downlighters were fitted as uplighters; lino was cracked; the fitter dropped a mug of Ovaltine on the stairs, ruined the kitchen wallpaper, split open his hand on the bath, broke the dishwasher, installed the shower so it emitted only hot or scalding water, left the loo leaking and with the flush broken, and botched the pump that operated the taps. 'This artistry took nine weeks to complete,' said Howers admiringly.

Medal for most heartfelt compassion

Present your breast Richard Branson. A fire wrecked Nicky Brindley's flat and injured her, but Virgin Media did not regard this as an adequate reason for moving home. When she tried to transfer her account to her temporary accommodation Virgin told her that she had effectively terminated her contract prematurely by changing address and must therefore pay a penalty of more than £200. It refused to transfer their account to the new address until this was done and refused to give her a migration authorisation code, which would have allowed her to find a friendlier provider.

Corporate efficiency award

All Jonathan Ouvry of London wanted to do was check whether Barclays had carried out an inter-bank transfer. After 30 minutes on the phone with a call-centre operative, the operative confessed himself baffled by his employer's procedures. Ouvry was not, he explained, allowed to speak to his branch direct and nor would that branch reply to a letter he had sent earlier because staff there open only registered mail. Unregistered letters are sent on to another destination for sorting, then relayed somewhere else. The transfer would have been authorised by a department somewhere in London that is unreachable by phone.

Best customer outreach
The prize goes to Removal Supply, the company from which Tobias Armbruester ordered 20 packing boxes. He never received them, nor did he get a reply to his calls and letters. When I asked the manager why, he told me: 'When people try to make out that their problems are mine and then ask for compensation . . . I bin [the letters].'

Jargon

Now you have reached the end of this book you will realise that companies do not wish to hear from you unless you have a credit card to hand. They might repel troublesome overtures by concealing their contact details or by confounding you with automated telephone systems. Should you successfully penetrate their defences you must be forearmed, for customer services staff may duck and weave and neutralise your complaint with specialised jargon, otherwise known as fob-offs. Here are some of the most common examples, along with appropriate translations:

'The system won't allow it'
Your kind of complaint isn't listed in my options, and I haven't a clue which button to press.

'That's against our policy'
This usually applies to requests to speak to a manager or to be transferred to a complaints department. Related to the above.

'I'm not allowed to under the Data Protection Act
The law as reinterpreted by customer services staff to thwart customers who ask for a manager's name or wish to discuss the account of a newly deceased partner.

'I'm not allowed to because of Health and Safety'
Similar to the above. Companies hope this will get them out of collecting a faulty mattress, disconnecting a washing machine or delivering a cooker to an upstairs flat.

Your complaint has been passed to the relevant department'
I've dumped it in the inbox of the absentee colleague at the next desk. Don't blame me if you never get a reply.

'Breakdown in communications'
It was too much trouble to get back to you.

'I'll get someone to call you back'
Get off the phone now, it's my lunch break.

'Our computers are down'
and I'll be in Majorca when you call back.

'Goodwill gesture'
We know we've screwed up but we have no intention of admitting it. Hopefully this £10 credit note will silence you.

'Credit note or voucher'
A canny means to coerce mistreated customers into spending more money with an offending company.

'We don't do refunds'
Surely no one has really read the Sale of Goods Act.

'You'll have to take it up with the manufacturer'
Ditto the above.

'We can't help because it's out of warranty/our 28 day complaints period'
Ditto ditto.

'We have no record of your complaint'
We were too inept to log your first call/we are suffering deliberate myopia and can't see it on our screen. Either way, we hope to persuade you that you are a fantasist.

'We've never received any complaints before'
Similar to the above. The idea is: be embarrassed, loser.

'We've been upgrading our systems'
All-encompassing excuse to explain deceased broadband service, hijacked gas accounts, melodramatic bills and vanished orders.

'We're a no-frills airline'
A useful opt-out when passengers demand wheelchair transport, a reunion with their luggage or a refund for a cancelled flight.

Tips for a successful complaint

Most large companies are inundated with complaints, some fanciful, some serious. No matter how important your complaint is to you, it will just be added to a miserable tally overseen by a stressed-out customer services worker, so to be sure that it makes the maximum impact you must know how to air your grievances effectively. An abusive scrawl on a ragged sheet of notepaper will be shunted to the back of the queue, whereas a lucid, properly addressed letter containing all the essential information is far more likely to prompt a response. Follow the steps below and you are more likely to get problems sorted effectively.

Make sure that your complaint is valid
If early termination charges prevent you from defecting to a cheaper mobile service provider, tough. You should have read the small print and realised that you are committed to a specific contract. If, however, you have received poor or non-existent service you are justified in requesting early release.

Work out what you want to achieve
Do you want a refund, replacement, compensation or simply an apology. If it's the first you have to act quickly or else you will lose your entitlement.

If you complain by telephone
Keep a note of whom you spoke to and when, and follow up the call with a letter reiterating your complaint and the telephone response. Do the same if your complaint is sent by a company's own webmail so that you have a record of it. Consumer Direct (www.consumerdirect.gov.uk) publishes template letters covering various categories of complaint.

Always address a letter to a specific person
It's best to start with the customer services manager. (If you aim too high – say, the chief executive – you'll suffer a delay while your letter is passed back down the ranks.) Find out the manager's name first and use their full title – Mr, Mrs or Ms.

Include your details
Remember to include your full name, address and any account, order or reference numbers, preferably near the top of the letter. If a company cannot easily find you on their systems they may leave you in limbo.

Check the correct address to send it to
Many larger organisations publish their in-house complaints procedures on their websites. Others should

show an address for head office or customer services.
Otherwise, ring and ask.

Do your homework
Mug up on consumer law and quote the relevant
regulation so that you can show that you know your
rights. If a faulty cooker breaches the Sale of Goods
Act 1979 say so.

Have the courage of your own convictions
Don't say that you think that a shambolic delivery
company may be in breach of the Supply of Goods &
Services Act 1982. Declare that it is.

Keep copies
Photocopy all relevant documents, such as receipts,
bank statements, order forms and advertisements, and
attach them to back up your complaint. If you are
seeking redress for a leaking boiler or a new, but soiled
sofa include a photo of the damage.

Suppress your literary instincts
Letters should be concise. Avoid capital letters, irate
underlinings, meandering detours and rhyming
couplets. Above all, avoid green ink. In addition,
restrain yourself from detailing over several pages the
effect the stress has had on your sciatica, love life or
dependent mother-in-law. This will only bore and
irritate and detract from the legal basis of your claim.

Check your spelling
Poorly written letters suggest that you are as sloppy as the company you are complaining about.

Be polite and reasonable
Whether you are writing or telephoning stay calm. Intemperate outpourings will give companies an excuse to refuse to deal with you.

Name names
If you mention the unhelpful attitude of, say, a shop manager or customer services operative, try to include their names.

Don't make unreasonable demands
Expecting £500 because a delivery was a day late will look like opportunism.

Don't apologise
Embarrassing as it may be for we British to complain, don't apologise. The grievance is all yours and the company should be grateful to you for pointing it out.

Set a deadline
Give the company a deadline for sending a useful response – 14 days is fair. Make a note of the date so that you can increase the pressure if it is missed.

Make sure your complaint arrives
Send all letters by recorded or special delivery so that

the firm cannot deny receiving them, and keep a log of whom you wrote or spoke to and when.

Get it in writing

Insist on written confirmation of anything that is promised to you over the phone.

Taking the next step

If your letter is ignored or inadequately dealt with you can escalate your complaint via, in turn, the managing director, chairman and chief executive. It's also worth copying in any relevant trade association or watchdog (if the company is a member of a trade association its logo should appear on their website) and, as a last resort, announcing that you intend to take legal action if you do not receive a satisfactory response within, say, a month.

Don't be fobbed off by lame excuses

If a company demands a receipt – for a faulty item for instance – you are not legally required to produce one. A bank or credit card statement showing the payment will do. Nor can the company claim that you should have complained within 28 days. You have up to six years to lodge a grievance regardless of warranty periods. If a shop refers you to the manufacturer remind them of the law, which states that your contract is with the retailer.

If, after a reasonable deadline, you have made no progress consult Consumer Direct (08454 040506 www.consumerdirect.gov.uk) on your rights and options. The website includes template letters covering various categories of complaint and the regulations that govern them.

Complaining to an ombudsman

If the company is a member of an ombudsman scheme and sent you a letter of deadlock, abused its own complaints procedures or failed to respond within a certain timescale, you can refer your complaint free to independent arbitrators.

When all else fails

You have two options. If an item or service cost more than £100 and you paid by credit card you can request a refund from your card issuer, which is held jointly liable with the trader for breaches of contract under the Consumer Credit Act 1974. Visa also offers similar protection but without the £100 payment limit to its card holders, both credit and debit as long as they apply within 120 days. This scheme is not well known, even among bank staff, so be persistent.

The small claims court is the second option, but only if you can produce a good reason for not using an arbitration or mediation scheme and if your claim is for £5,000 or less. It's probably not worth taking court action if your opponent is bankrupt (ask the Insolvency Service on 020 7637 1110; 21 Bloomsbury St, London WC1B 3SS) or if they have previous unpaid court orders. You can find this out for a small fee at www.registry-trust.org.uk or by writing to Registry Trust Ltd, 173–175 Cleveland St, London W1T 6QR.

You can start a small claim online at www.moneyclaim.gov.uk or at any county court in England and Wales. Contact details will be under Courts in the telephone directory or at www.hmcourts-service.gov.uk In Scotland small claims are £3,000 or less and are started at the sheriff court. The small claims track is more of an arbitration than a full court hearing – you don't need a solicitor – but its judgments are legally enforceable. Unless you are on benefits, pension or a low income you will have to pay an up-front fee calculated according to the amount you are claiming, and if your opponent defends the case you may incur further costs for travel, witness expenses and the like. You might get these back if you win.

If your claim is for more that £5,000 (£3,000 in Scotland) you will probably require a full court hearing. Consult your local Citizens Advice Bureau (www.citizensadvice.org.uk) first to find out if the hassle and expense are worth it.

Useful contacts

Consumer advice bodies

Citizens Advice Bureau
www.citizensadvice.org.uk
   Trained advisers will help with legal, financial and consumer problems face to face or by telephone. You can find your local bureau on the website.

Consumer Action Group
www.consumeractiongroup.co.uk
   Online forums give advice on any consumer issue.

Consumer Direct
www.consumedirect.gov.uk 08454 040506
   Deals directly with consumer queries and offers wide-ranging advice on buying goods and services on its website.

www.moneymadeclear.fsa.gov.uk
   Consumer advice on money matters from the Financial Services Authority.

Trading Standards Institute www.tradingstandards.gov.uk
This has a consumer advice section on buying goods and services. It doesn't deal direct with consumer enquiries, but will do a postcode search for your local trading standards office.

UK European Consumer Centre
www.ukecc.net 08456 04 05 03
Provides information on consumer rights in Europe and assists in cross-border disputes.

Which?
www.which.co.uk 01992 822800
The home of the campaigning consumer organisation can't help individually, but has advice sheets on most consumer issues. Its Best Buy scheme accredits the best products and services. Subscribers can find product comparisons and reviews.

Consumer protection services

www.buywithconfidence.gov.uk
A register of traders vetted and approved by trading standards officials. You can search by postcode and category.

www.trustmark.org.uk
Similar to above. A government-endorsed scheme to accredit reliable traders.

Safe Buy

www.safebuy.org.uk 01491 411 111

A quality assurance scheme for web-based retailers. It offers mediation if there is a dispute with a member trader.

Fax Preference Scheme

www.fpsonline.org.uk 020 7291 3330

It's already illegal to send unsolicited faxes to private individuals, so this is aimed mainly at businesses, but householders can sign up too.

Mailing Preference Scheme

www.mpsonline.org.uk 020 7291 3310

Same as the Telephone Preference Scheme, but it stems the tide of junk mail, except for circulars addressed to The Occupier. To opt out of these write to Freepost RRBT-ZBXB-TTTS, Royal Mail Door to Door Opt Outs, Kingsmead House, Oxpens Road, Oxford OX1 1RX, or email optout@royalmail.com

Telephone Preference Service

www.tpsonline.org.uk 020 7291 3320

Run by the direct marketing industry, it will protect you from unsolicited sales calls. Once you are signed up it is illegal for firms to telephone you without your consent.

Air Travel Organisers' Licensing
www.atol.org.uk 020 7453 6350

A financial protection scheme for holiday packages involving air travel. Always check that a tour operator is ATOL registered.

Watchdogs

Air Transport Users Council
www.auc.org.uk 020 7240 6061

Funded by the Civil Aviation Authority, its website summarises passenger rights. It offers individual advice and will mediate if a complaint about an airline cannot be resolved.

Consumer Council for Water
www.ccwater.org.uk 0121 345 1000

A statutory body to champion consumer interests. It will take up complaints that cannot be satisfactorily resolved with a water company.

Consumer Focus
www.consumerfocus.org.uk 020 77997900

A merger of the National Consumer Council, Postwatch and Energywatch. It only investigates energy- or postal-related complaints from vulnerable customers and does not provide direct advice, but there is an overview of rights of energy and postal customers on its website.

Passenger Focus
www.passengerfocus.org.uk 0300 123 2350

A government-funded body that represents the interests of train, bus and coach passengers. Advice on consumer rights is published on the website, and it may take up a complaint if it has not been resolved by the transport company.

Ombudsmen and arbitration schemes

British & Irish Ombudsman Association
www.bioa.org.uk 020 8894 9272

It doesn't handle complaints directly, but lists ombudsman services and other bodies that do.

Communications & Internet Services Adjudication Scheme
www.cisas.org.uk 020 7520 3827

An Ofcom-approved alternative dispute resolution scheme for telecoms complaints against member companies.

Dispute Resolution Services
www.idrs.ltd.uk 020 7520 3800

A subsidiary of the Chartered Insititute of Arbitrators that runs over 80 consumer redress services.

Energy Ombudsman
www.energy-ombudsman.org.uk 0330 440 1624 or
01925 530 263

It will sort out disputes between gas and electricity firms and customers.

Financial Ombudsman Service
www.financial-ombudsman.org.uk 0845 080 1800
It will take up unresolved complaints about banks, insurers and finance firms and offers advice on its website.

Furniture Ombudsman
www.fira.co.uk 01438 777700 (advice line 08701 620 690)
Independent standards organisation for furniture and floor coverings. It will help resolve disputes with member companies.

Office of the Telecommunications Ombudsman
www.otelo.org.uk 0330 440 1614 or 01925 430 049
An Ofcom-approved alternative dispute resolution scheme for telecoms complaints against member companies.

The Property Ombudsman Service
www.tpos.co.uk 01722 333306
Since October 2008 all estate agents must be registered with one of two approved redress schemes – this one or the Surveyors Ombudsman service.

Removals Industry Ombudsman Scheme
www.removalsombudsman.org.uk 01753 888206
It will take on unresolved complaints about member removals firms, including all members of the National Guild of Removers and Storers.

Surveyors Ombudsman Service
www.surveyors-ombudsman.org.uk 01925 530270

Regulators

Consumers cannot usually complain directly to a regulator, but it is good to know who they are because they can offer useful advice or direct you towards appropriate avenues for complaint.

Advertising Standards Authority
www.asa.org.uk 020 7492 2222
Upholds advertising standards and cracks down on misleading advertisements. There is a complaints form on its website.

Information Commissioner
www.ico.gov.uk 01625 545700
It enforces the Data Protection Act. Its website outlines individuals' rights under the law.

Financial Services Authority
www.fsa.gov.uk 020 7066 1000
The FSA regulates the financial industry. Its related website www.moneymadeclear.fsa.gov.uk provides financial advice for consumers.

Ofcom
www.ofcom.gov.uk 020 7981 3040 or 0300 123 3333
Regulates telecoms, TV and radio. It will consider

complaints from individual consumers, and its website offers consumer advice.

Office of Fair Trading
www.oft.gov.uk 08457 22 44 99

Its slogan is 'making markets work well for consumers'. It enforces competition and consumer protection law. You can report a business that does not comply with consumer legislation, but it won't investigate individual complaints.

Ofwat
www.ofwat.gov.uk 0121 625 1300

Regulates water and sewerage companies in England and Wales and sets compensation levels for consumers in its Guaranteed Standards of Service.

Office of the Gas and Electricity Markets
www.ofgem.gov.uk 020 7901 7295

Promotes competition within the energy market.

Phonepay Plus
www.phonepayplus.org.uk 0800 500 212

Formerly ICSTIS, it regulates premium-rate phone services and deals with related customer complaints.

Trade associations

Some of these associations offer consumer mediation services. All enforce a code of practice, and most publish advice and information for customers.

Association of British Insurers
www.abi.org.uk 020 7600 3333
  The voice of the insurance industry. Consumer advice
  leaflets are available on its website.

Association of British Travel Agents
www.abta.com 020 3117 0500
  Its members, which include hundreds of tour
  operators, are governed by a code of practice, and
  an arbitration scheme is available for discontented
  customers of signed-up companies.

Association of Independent Tour Operators
www.aito.co.uk 020 8744 9280
  This offers a mediation scheme for a fee, which is
  refunded if the mediators find in favour of the
  customer.

Association of Manufacturers of Domestic Appliances
www.amdea.org.uk 020 7405 0666
  It has an FAQ section for consumers and a directory
  of manufacturers.

Association for Payment Clearing Services
www.apacs.org.uk 020 7711 6200
  Represents companies that deliver payment services
  for customers. Its FAQs section covers a range of
  payment queries, from cheque clearance to identity
  fraud.

Association of Plumbing and Heating Contractors
www.aphc.co.uk 0121 711 5030

> It vets its members, which must abide by a code of practice, and it offers a directory of accredited tradespeople.

British Association of Removers
www.bar.co.uk 01923 699 480

> Its members are bound by a code of practice, and it offers a conciliation scheme in case of complaints.

British Bankers Association
www.bba.org.uk

> It oversees a code of practice binding member companies and publishes consumer advice on its website.

British Vehicle Rental and Leasing Association
www.bvrla.co.uk 01494 434747

> It offers consumer tips and a conciliation service.

Building Societies Association
www.bsa.org.uk 020 7520 5900

> Its consumer section includes fact sheets, advice and a helpline.

Chartered Institute of Plumbing and Heating Engineering
www.ciphe.org.uk 01708 472791

> A find-a-plumber directory plus top tips and a mediation service.

Confederation of Roofing Contractors
www.corc.co.uk 01206 306600
> Protects the public from cowboy roofers. An online directory identifies approved roofers by area.

Direct Marketing Association
www.mydm.co.uk 0845 703 4599
> This is the website for consumers, with FAQs and information on sales overtures from companies.

Energy Retail Association
www.energy-retail.org.uk 020 7104 4150
> Its members are the Big Six energy suppliers, which have evolved their own common code of practice. The website offers advice for consumers on utility issues.

Federation of Master Builders
www.fmb.org.uk 020 7242 7583
> The website contains advice on home improvements, a directory of approved builders, a jargon buster and a dispute resolution service.

Internet Service Providers Association
www.ispa.org.uk 0870 050 0710
> Offers consumer advice and will take on unresolved complaints about member companies.

Kitchen, Bathroom, Bedroom Specialists Association
www.kbsa.org.uk 01623 818808
> Consumer advice leaflets are on the website together

with a postcode search facility for vetted members. Deposits with member companies are protected by an in-house insurance scheme.

National Association of Estate Agents
www.naea.co.uk 01926 496800

The website contains consumer advice on buying, selling or renting, and there is a mediation service available if things go wrong with a member company.

Painting and Decorating Association
www.paintingdecoratingassociation.co.uk 024 7635 3776

Members are vetted and must have at least five years' experience as well as liability insurance. A postcode search will find local professionals. There's also a mediation service.

Passenger Shipping Association
www.the-psa.co.uk 020 7436 2449

It bonds member cruise and ferry companies and offers a conciliation service.

Radio, Electrical and Television Retailers Association
www.retra.co.uk 01234 269110

Represents 1,400 independent retailers, which are bound by a code of practice. Useful consumer advice and FAQs on the website together with a postcode search.

Solar Trade Association
www.solar-trade.org.uk 01908 442290
It regulates its members and answers consumer queries about solar power.

The Society of Tickets Agents and Retailers
www.S-T-A-R.org.uk 0870 603 9011
Its members are bound by a code of practice, and it will investigate unresolved complaints.

Trade Association Forum
www.taforum.org 020 7395 8283
You can search a list of all trade associations by category or alphabetically.

When things get nasty

Her Majesty's Courts Service
www.hmcourts-service.gov.uk 0845 4568770
This explains how and when to start legal proceedings under the small claims track and has downloadable forms for commencing action.

www.moneyclaim.gov.uk
Part of HM Courts Service, it enables claimants to pursue a case online.

Registry Trust Ltd
www.registry-trust.org.uk 020 7380 0133
This will list any previous or unpaid county court

judgments against individuals and enable you to assess your chances of winning redress from your foe.

Companies House
www.companieshouse.gov.uk 0303 1234 500

Here you can check whether a company is still trading, find its registered address and previous trading names and, for a fee, learn the name and home address of the directors.

Laws you should know about

See the Department for Business, Innovation and Skills (www.berr.gov.uk) for more information.

Sale of Goods Act 1979

Traders must sell goods that are as described, fit for purpose and of satisfactory quality, otherwise customers can request a refund, repair, replacement or compensation.

The Sale and Supply of Goods to Consumers Regulations 2002

The regulations have slightly amended the above to harmonise the UK with EU law. They oblige traders to prove that goods were not inherently faulty within the first six months of purchase and make guarantees legally binding.

Supply of Goods and Services Act 1982

This requires traders to provide services to a proper standard using goods of satisfactory quality and to complete the work within a reasonable time and for a reasonable charge.

Consumer Credit Act 1974

The Act requires companies that offer goods or services on credit or lend money to be licensed by the Office of Fair Trading. Section 75 holds the card issuer jointly liable if a trader in the UK or overseas is in breach of contract and if the goods or services cost between £100 and £30,000. The Act also gives you the right to inspect your credit files for a £2 fee.

Consumer Protection (Distance Selling) Regulations 2000

Customers who shop by phone, TV, mail order or the internet must be given clear information about the goods, this information must be confirmed in writing, and they must be allowed seven working days to change their minds. It also offers protection from credit card fraud.

Consumer Protection Act 1987

More EU law to impose strict liability for damage caused by defective goods, to give the government powers to regulate the safety of consumer products and to make it a criminal offence to give misleading price information.

Consumer Protection from Unfair Trading Regulations 2008

The regulations amend the Trade Descriptions Act 1968 to harmonise unfair trading laws across the EU. They forbid companies to mislead consumers by actions or omissions or to use high-pressure sales techniques.

The Cancellation of Contracts Made in the Consumers Home or Place of Work etc. Regulations 2000

These give customers the right to cancel a contract for goods or services of £35 or more signed on their doorstep, even if the salesperson's visit was requested.

Data Protection Act 1998

The Act gives individuals some control over their personal information and imposes restrictions on how companies can use customers' data.

Unsolicited Goods and Services Act 1971

This makes it an offence for traders to send goods or provide services you have not ordered. You may keep unsolicited goods without payment unless the company collects them.

Unfair Terms in Consumer Contracts Regulations 1994 and 1999

The regulations forbid, among other things, companies to include clauses that would disproportionately benefit them to the detriment of the customer.

Misrepresentation Act 1967

This allows a customer to rescind a contract if the trader makes a false, incomplete or misleading statement to tempt them into signing.

Electronic Commerce (EC Directive) Regulations 2002

Internet and digital traders must state in a 'clear, comprehensible and unambiguous manner' the technical steps involved to place an order and must make clear terms and conditions. Traders must promptly acknowledge the order by electronic means and advise how to amend any input errors made.

Control of Misleading Advertisements Regulations 1988

The regulations require the Office of Fair Trading to investigate complaints about misleading ads.

The Package Travel Regulations 1992

These make the tour operator liable for failures of any component of a package holiday. They also give consumer rights if a holiday is significantly altered or cancelled.

Regulation (EC) 261/2004

This sets out passenger entitlements if they are downgraded or denied boarding, or if their flight is delayed or cancelled.

Athens Convention

An international treaty to set compensation levels

for loss or damage to passengers' luggage (or to passengers themselves) while on a cruise or ferry.

Montreal Convention
A treaty adopted by the International Civil Aviation Organisation that establishes an airline's liability for death or injury to passengers and loss, damage or delay to baggage.

Acknowledgments

Rachel Chorley, Ombudsman press office (TOSL)

Philip Cullum, Deputy Chief Executive, Consumer Focus

Simon Evans, Chief Executive Air Transport Users Council

Emma Parker, Manager media relations, Financial Services Ombudsman

David Sanders, Lead officer for civil law at the Trading Standards Institute

Bruce Treloar, lead officer on travel and holiday industry, Trading Standards Institute

Michelle Whiteman, Payments Council